The Flexible ELA Classroom

Find out how to differentiate your middle school ELA instruction so that all students can become better readers, writers, and critical thinkers. Author Amber Chandler invites you into her classroom and shows how you can adjust your lessons to suit different learning needs while still meeting state standards and keeping your students accountable. She provides a wide variety of helpful tools and strategies, ranging from easy options that you can try out immediately to deeper-integration ideas that will reshape your classroom as a flexible, personalized learning environment. Topics include:

- Using choice boards and menus to teach vocabulary, reading, and presentation skills in fun and interactive ways;
- Grouping students strategically to maximize learning outcomes and encourage collaboration;
- Making vocabulary learning interesting and memorable with visual aids, tiered lists, and personalized word studies;
- Designing your own Project Based Learning lessons to unleash your students' creativity;
- Assessing students' progress without the use of one-size-fits-all testing;
- And more!

Bonus: Downloadable versions of some of the rubrics and handouts in this book are available on the Routledge website at www.routledge.com/9781138681040. Also, check out the book's website, www.doyoudifferentiate.com, for additional articles and strategies.

Amber Chandler is a middle school teacher in the Frontier Central School District in New York. She is a frequent writer for MiddleWeb, ShareMyLesson, *AMLE Magazine*, and other educational resources.

Other Eye on Education Books Available from Routledge
(www.routledge.com/eyeoneducation)

History Class Revisited:
Tools and Projects to Engage Middle School Students in Social Studies
Jody Passanisi

The Genius Hour Guidebook:
Fostering Passion, Wonder, and Inquiry in the Classroom
Denise Krebs and Gallit Zvi

STEM by Design:
Strategies and Activities for Grades 4–8
Anne Jolly

Differentiated Instruction, Second Edition:
A Guide for World Language Teachers
Deborah Blaz

Infusing Grammar into the Writer's Workshop:
A Guide for K–6 Teachers
Amy Benjamin and Barbara Golub

Teaching the Common Core Literature Standards in Grades 2–5:
Strategies, Mentor Texts, and Units of Study
Lisa Morris

The Narrative Writing Toolkit:
Using Mentor Texts in Grades 3–8
Sean Ruday

The Argument Writing Toolkit:
Using Mentor Texts in Grades 6–8
Sean Ruday

The Informational Writing Toolkit:
Using Mentor Texts in Grades 3–5
Sean Ruday

The Flexible ELA Classroom

Practical Tools for Differentiated Instruction in Grades 4–8

Amber Chandler

First published 2017
by Routledge
711 Third Avenue, New York, NY 10017

and by Routledge
2 Park Square, Milton Park, Abingdon, Oxon, OX14 4RN

Routledge is an imprint of the Taylor & Francis Group, an informa business

© 2017 Amber Chandler

The right of Amber Chandler to be identified as author of this work has been asserted by her in accordance with sections 77 and 78 of the Copyright, Designs and Patents Act 1988.

All rights reserved. No part of this book may be reprinted or reproduced or utilised in any form or by any electronic, mechanical, or other means, now known or hereafter invented, including photocopying and recording, or in any information storage or retrieval system, without permission in writing from the publishers.

Trademark notice: Product or corporate names may be trademarks or registered trademarks, and are used only for identification and explanation without intent to infringe.

Library of Congress Cataloging-in-Publication Data
Names: Chandler, Amber, author.
Title: The flexible ELA classroom : practical tools for differentiated instruction in grades 4–8 / by Amber Chandler.
Description: New York, NY : Routledge, 2016. | Includes bibliographical references.
Identifiers: LCCN 2016018575 | ISBN 9781138681033 (hardback) | ISBN 9781138681040 (pbk.) | ISBN 9781315564234 (e-book)
Subjects: LCSH: English language—Study and teaching (Middle school) | Language arts (Middle school) | Individualized instruction.
Classification: LCC LB1631 .C4468 2016 | DDC 428.0071/2—dc23
LC record available at https://lccn.loc.gov/2016018575

ISBN: 978-1-138-68103-3 (hbk)
ISBN: 978-1-138-68104-0 (pbk)
ISBN: 978-1-315-56423-4 (ebk)

Typeset in Palatino
by Apex CoVantage, LLC

Contents

Companion Website vi
Meet the Author vii
Acknowledgments viii
Introduction xi

1   **Options and Choice: The Heart of Differentiation** 1

2   **Strategic Groupings: Flexibility for Student Engagement** 30

3   **Word Study: Personalizing Vocabulary** 57

4   **Project Based Learning: Differentiating Student
    Learning Experiences** 74

5   **Assessment: Valuing the Individual in a
    Standardized World** 110

6   **Family Partnerships: Creating a Customized
    "Dream Team" for Students** 123

    A Final Thought 137
    Bibliography 138

Companion Website

The following rubrics and handouts from the book are also available on the Routledge website as free eResources:

Rubric for Class Novel Projects	page 21
Presentation Menu Options	page 26
The Giver Pre-Reading Fishbowl Notes	page 40
Personal Vocabulary	page 69
Passion Project Parameters	page 101
Process Presentation Rubric	page 105
School and Family Team Meeting Form	page 134

The eResources are indicated in the book by the eResources logo. You can access the eResources by visiting the book product page: www.routledge.com/9781138681040. Click on the tab that says "eResources" and select the files. They will begin downloading to your computer.

In addition, bonus articles and strategies are available on the book's website, www.doyoudifferentiate.com.

Meet the Author

Amber Chandler is a National Board Certified middle school ELA teacher in Hamburg, New York, with a Master's Degree in Literature as well as a School Building Leader certification. Amber has enjoyed a wide variety of teaching opportunities—from 6th grade remediation, to college courses, to education workshops on differentiation, Danielson's Domains, and Project Based Learning. No matter which level Amber is teaching, the goal is always the same: Engage students to take charge of their own learning.

Amber's blogs and articles have appeared in MiddleWeb, ShareMyLesson, Getting Smart, ASCD's "Ideas From the Field," Moms Rising, the EdVocate, *AMLE Magazine*, and *New York Teacher*. She has served as a co-moderator for the #WhatIsSchool education chat, as well as initiating the first #NYEdVoice Twitter chat when she was a New York Educators Voice Fellow. Amber has appeared as a guest on BAM! Radio Network to discuss the benefits of Project Based Learning, as well as webcasts for AMLE on the importance of teaching speaking and listening skills, and how to use artifacts to improve teacher evaluation in APPRs.

Amber was chosen from a nationwide search as one of a handful of panelists for Fordham's "Evaluating the Content and Quality of Next Generation Assessments" to evaluate how state assessments compare in their ability to assess Common Core Standards. She's also served as a School Review Team member, offering her observations and expertise, particularly in the area of Project Based Learning.

Amber is an active member of the American Federation of Teachers (AFT) as a ShareMyLesson Ambassador and participant in the Resource and Materials Development at the Summer Educators Academy. Amber also is a featured contributor for the AFT blog, "Classroom Voices." She serves as the Head Building Representative for her local, Frontier Central Teachers Association.

Acknowledgments

Sometimes in life, we have cheerleaders, those special people who watch and encourage us along the way. I was lucky enough nearly twenty years ago to have three great mentors to begin my teaching career at Portsmouth High School in New Hampshire—Mary Potter, Sherry Fawcett, and Paula Bruno. These women were so excited for me at every turn, making sure to share their collective "do's and don'ts" while making me laugh and keeping it all in perspective. If you were to peek in my classroom, the influence of these amazing educators would be clear in the respect I have for my students, the love I have for literature, and the passion I have for teaching writing. It is because of them that I mentor as many new teachers as possible because I realize that teaching can either be a lonely business or the most collaborative and fulfilling profession imaginable.

Other times, we have people who call us out when we need it, are all about the tough love, and are a great source of strength when we aren't sure what to do. I've been lucky enough to have Denise Konieczko, Angela Ford, Sissy Emery, and Judy Crawford around when I needed to hear from women who are, in their own right, amazingly strong and who have never been afraid to fight for what is right. Whenever I wondered, "Do I really want to get myself tangled up in this?" I could look to these women, who inevitably would say, "If it matters, you sure do."

I've been lucky enough to have another sort of people in my life who refuse to believe that I have any limitations. My dad, Gene Crawford; my husband, Matt Chandler; and my mentor, Dr. Peter Loehr, always listen to whatever my next plan happens to be and say, "Why not? Of course you can," without an ounce of trepidation. I've sometimes grown frustrated with their perpetual expectation that I can do anything, but it is from their confidence in me that I have developed into the educator and writer I am today. My husband keeps me laughing, and though I never let him read a word before it is published, he always tells me it's brilliant, which always helps.

In the last few years, writing has become more than a hobby, and that is because of some really amazing people who were willing to let me say my piece. Only a few years ago, Heidi Glidden, when I asked if I could write a weekly blog for ShareMyLesson, said yes, and that single word has changed my life, as I was off and running. Pat George and Dru Tomlin at *AMLE Magazine*, Ami Turner and Natalie Dean at ShareMyLesson, and especially John Norton and Susan Curtis at MiddleWeb have been crucial figures in my "writing life." John, especially, helped me to understand my writer's voice and that the ability to bring readers into my classroom is something special and worth sharing.

Of course, my students and their parents are so important to me, and there is nothing more satisfying than to watch students learn from each other and pursue their passions. I can't thank my "kiddos," as I call them, enough because they are the ones who inspire me to try new things—like figure out how to have a paperless classroom and build websites. It is my students' fearlessness that makes me want to do better by them and make their learning experiences worthy of their attention. Families are so crucial to a child's success, and I appreciate every partnership I've experienced, and I want to thank the parents who lend me their children.

I couldn't imagine writing this book without the support and encouragement of Team 8Blue. These teachers care more about the whole student than any other people I know, and for that, I am grateful. When a committed group of teachers collaborate, amazing things can happen. I especially want to thank Laura Klein and Mary Regula, my co-teachers (and occasionally my co-conspirators!) for always saying "Sure" when I come up with something on the way to school that I just have to try out. It is their willingness to bend that has allowed me, finally, to create the kind of flexible classroom that I believe is best for students. Rachel Brew, our school Library Media Specialist, has encouraged me to try new things with my students, and her willingness to share her expertise and space with us has made all the difference. I truly could not do what I do without her support.

Interestingly, in this digital world where you "e-meet" people, some of my major influences are people I have never met in person. Lauren Davis, my editor, has been with me for every twist and turn of writing this book, letting me pick her brain and responding to my ongoing questions. It was immediately clear that she had a teacher's heart and could bring the best out in my writing. Not only has she held my hand, she has completely spoiled me with constant communication and encouragement along the way. And, obviously there could not be a book about differentiation that does not acknowledge the profound impact of Carol Tomlinson, Rick Wormeli, and Robert Marzano. I am so grateful that

I stumbled upon these gurus when I needed them most, and it completely blows my mind that this book is my foray into the ongoing conversation about differentiation.

Finally, I must thank my own children. Zoey is, believe it or not, at ten years old, quite the aficionado concerning differentiation and Project Based Learning because since the beginning she's been reading my writing before I send it along. She is my best critic because she is willing to tell me when I don't sound like myself or say something that doesn't line up with her idea of me, which keeps me both humble and honest. My son, Oliver, is a different kind of inspiration because it was in watching him design entire worlds for his trains and LEGO that made me realize that he was creating a narrative—a hands-on, fully involved experience that was far more complex than the essays that I was assigning, and I was able to see that students learn best when they are passionate about what they are learning and can grow in ways that I could never imagined. Thanks to my children who made me see that the best laid plans will never measure up to the magic that children can create for themselves.

Introduction

My Journey to a Differentiated Classroom

"Sit anywhere," I'd say as the class filed in. I wanted my classroom to be a place where everyone was free to express themselves as we talked about Whitman, Emerson, and Thoreau. I didn't stand in front of the room or sit at my teacher's desk. Instead, I sat with my students in a circle. My room was decorated with purposefully ironic ABC charts (I was teaching AP Literature) and quotes I thought were important scrawled on colored paper. I'd play rainforest sounds while everyone found a seat. I had chimes. Many of my students called me Amber, and I was the advisor of *Epitome*, the high school literary magazine. I fancied myself quite the freethinker, in my Birkenstocks with wool socks and overalls. As much as this sounds like a *Saturday Night Live* skit, this worked. The reason I was given the freedom to do things my way was that I got the results the school wanted: I always had higher than an 80% pass rate for the AP Literature exam, and even then, nearly two decades ago, that held weight.

My students, who were only a few years younger than me, looked up to me like a cool big sister and loved to listen to me talk about the grad classes I was still taking. Those students are now my Facebook friends, and occasionally they'll tag me in a grammar meme or quote a line from *A Prayer for Owen Meany* or *Catcher in the Rye*. I was rigorous before it was a thing, not because someone told me to be, but because I loved literature, and talking about books all day was a dream come true. I shared my writing with my students, and they were receptive to my suggestions about theirs. They knew I had just graduated from college, and they were all in the top 20% and wanted every morsel of advice and information that could help them along the way.

Those first idyllic students were coming to me in the AP Literature class from affluent families who were second and third generation in the area, had webs of support systems, and had to have been recommended by their English teacher after junior year and maintain a "B" average. When something proved difficult, these families had tutors on speed dial. Most of the college recommendations I wrote were for Harvard or MIT or the New York Film Institute, or other private colleges with huge price tags. In fact, not once did I write a recommendation in those years for a community college. Some used University of New Hampshire as their "safe" school, but these kids had clearly been groomed from kindergarten to be the college students they were soon to be. I delivered content, and I was very good at it. Teaching seemed remarkably simple, and I was loving every minute of it. Soon, I got married, received my tenure, bought a house, and settled in for a smooth sail.

As you may have guessed, the story doesn't end like that, or I wouldn't have a book to write. My husband's job took us to Buffalo, New York, and I found myself at an interview for a middle school ELA position. I had not applied for this position; I had applied at the high school, but my application had made its way into a middle school pile somewhere along the line—back when there was an actual paper application to pass around. My husband made me go to the interview – "for practice," he'd said. It was probably because I wasn't even a tad nervous, since I obviously was never going to teach middle school, that I landed the job. I was going to teach 6th, 7th, and 8th grade ELA remediation. *I didn't know then, and it took me a few years, but I was about to learn the difference between teaching content and teaching students.*

Spoiler alert: You've probably already figured out that I was going to need more than an interesting personality and love for literature to impress middle school students, much less teach them ELA. I'd been told that these were students who struggled with ELA and who had not been identified as Special Education students, but many of them would likely end up with a 504. Ashamed as I am to admit it now, that information didn't mean much, given my prior experience. In fairness, the first thing I did after I was hired was head straight to a bookstore to see what I could find to help me know what to do, because I was scared of these little people.

I probably wouldn't have lasted in middle school if not by divine intervention in the form of Rick Wormeli's *Meet Me in the Middle*. I pretty much believed it was written for me, just as I've heard other teachers say. As I stood in the bookstore, I almost laughed out loud to read in the forward what Ed Brazee chose to open with: "Let me say this simply—teachers need this book." As a poor-ish young teacher, I could afford one book, and this one seemed like destiny. The sailing wasn't going to be smooth, but I had a map!

I learned what I was supposed to do, but differentiation was a new word to me, and I was still in the one-size-fits-all mindset perpetuated by higher education at the time. After the first few weeks, I remember saying to my husband, "I know English. I know literature. These kids just don't care." My husband is painfully aware of my cerebral qualities, and gingerly asked, "Why don't you get to know them first?" Since I didn't have any better ideas, my husband's advice became a part of my game plan for my first year teaching middle school: just get to know them.

My students were gracious and forgiving, as I continually ran out of time because I didn't get the pacing. They were tolerant when I had to keep looping back mid-sentence to rephrase because I had forgotten I was talking to eleven-year-olds who struggled with reading, not students on their way to an Ivy League school. My students helped me learn to laugh at myself as I repeatedly messed up our every-other-day schedule, and the new teacher problem of having to meet in different rooms. They made it easy, but I still didn't feel like I was teaching well.

Luckily, I was able to push into classes to see how middle school teachers were simply miracle workers. I couldn't believe how much happened in the short forty-minute class period! Around November, I realized that not only did I need to get to know the middle school students, but I also needed to understand strategies that met their needs. I will always be grateful for the opportunity I had to see how teachers approached reaching students of so many different abilities and maturity levels. Through these experiences, I learned how to use choice boards, menu options, and a whole magician's hat full of differentiation tricks. The chapters mirror my own forays into differentiation, beginning with the easiest to implement, all the way to really challenging (but rewarding!) shifts in mindset and classroom structure. In the coming chapters, you'll get to "push in" to my classroom and see the ways I differentiate, and through this close-up view you'll identify ways you want to incorporate these strategies and philosophies into your own practice.

The Roadmap: What You'll Find in This Book

The book, in a sense, is my journey from "cookie cutter compliance" as a newbie teacher to appreciating the needs of all students as I grew more confident. You'll see my first foray (which got me hooked!) into differentiation in Chapter 1, "Options and Choice: The Heart of Differentiation," and you'll find easy options to get started right away. Chapter 2, "Strategic Grouping: Flexibility for Student Engagement," explains how I transformed my classroom—physically, emotionally, socially, and academically—into a space for all types of learners. Chapter 3, "Word Study: Personalizing Vocabulary," is a collection of tools I've discovered to improve retention and avoid the dreaded vocabulary list to memorize; you'll be able to implement these ideas immediately. Chapter 4, "Project Based Learning: Differentiating Student Learning Experiences," might be where you'd say I lost my traditional approach to teaching almost entirely, and I set out to facilitate student-centered learning experiences that naturally differentiate.

It was around this point in my evolution as an educator that I realized that the common factor in my attempts to reach all students was flexibility. If I allowed students to pursue their own interests, I was going to need to let go of so many constraints. As I've written this book, it has occurred to me that yes, this is a book about differentiation, but it is also a book about an attitude—a "whatever it takes" approach that requires a culture of flexibility, and I've realized that at the center of this is a giant analogy. You'd expect no less from an English teacher, right? A flexible classroom bends and sways with the "next thing" and stays rooted in the belief that all students can and want to learn, but that learning might look very different for each student; it doesn't mean that I abandon standards, and students are required to "show what they know."

Project Based Learning is the most challenging to implement, but I provide tips and resources to help you make the leap. Chapter 5, "Assessment: Valuing the Individual in a Standardized World," is my response to the politicization of learning, and it provides many ways for teachers to measure student learning that do not involve coloring in bubbles; however, I live in a reality that requires answer sheets, and most of you do too, so I provide strategies to help students approach testing. Finally, Chapter 6, "Family Partnerships: Creating a Customized 'Dream Team' for Students," is the payoff. I firmly believe that I can encourage deep relationships with families when I am positive I am doing what is best for students—one by one. It is my sincere wish that these tools will help you on your own journey as well.

1

Options and Choice

The Heart of Differentiation

I first dipped my toe in the water of differentiation after seeing other teachers use choice boards. Choice boards are graphic organizers that offer students different options for activities to complete, therefore allowing students to have a say in their learning. These graphic organizers may be used in various ways—to front-load background knowledge, to formatively assess, or as the final assessment. Many contain nine boxes, like Tic-Tac-Toe boards, but there is a wide variety of possible formats. I was intrigued by choice boards because they seemed easy to implement—my biggest concern early on. It turns out that choice boards are an excellent entry point into differentiation because they are predictable for the teacher and engaging for students. Choice boards can be used for both fiction and non-fiction, and with a variety of standards. They can also be designed fairly simply (such as the nine-choice Tic-Tac-Toe board) or can be elaborately designed. Eventually you'll leap almost instinctively from choice boards to menus for differentiation, since menus can be more complex and allow you to add more to the student experience. The best part about the choice board and menu strategies is that they stay relevant year after year, and they can be reimagined to meet the needs of each wave of students. In the next pages, we'll look at how to implement these strategies, and I'll offer plenty of examples.

> **Sneak Peek**
>
> This chapter shows . . .
> - *why choice boards are a great tool for providing options*
> - *how to use choice boards to teach vocabulary and reading*
> - *how to use choice boards to incorporate Bloom's taxonomy and 21st-century skills*
> - *why menus can be useful for differentiating instruction*
> - *how to use menus to teach novels, independent reading, and presentations*

Choice Boards

Choice boards allow teachers to differentiate in three ways: content, process, and product. The content may be targeted to grade level, accelerated, remediated, or enriched. The process is able to take into account learning styles, Bloom's taxonomy, multiple intelligences, 21st-century skills, and the individual talents and passions of your students. The product—the way students "show what they know"—is simply a delivery method to demonstrate what students learn. Choice boards allow students to express their learning in a variety of ways, and as a bonus, teachers aren't grading the same cookie cutter answers, over and over.

There is no end to variety when it comes to choice boards. When creating a choice board you should be guided by the most important elements of the unit you are teaching, as well as the secondary skills you may want to reinforce. For example, you might create a choice board about a novel that has many options involving figurative language, a skill you have previously taught but want to spiral back into your curriculum. Teachers can create choice boards based on *their priorities for their students*, but the boards should be organized around themes. A teacher could create a board based on a combination of written/verbal/tactile/visual activities that addresses student ability and interest, coupled with the academic goals you have for your students.

Choice boards engage students in learning that is meaningful for them, while also meeting the requirements that you, the teacher, have set forth for them. This empowers students to make their own decisions and even learn to advocate for themselves. The choice boards aren't the instruction; they are the method by which students demonstrate the learning that has occurred, while still offering them the learning experience of presenting. One of the first things you'll notice is that using choice boards enhances instruction and learning because, when students set a purpose for their learning, their engagement increases.

Of course, there will always be some people—other teachers or parents—who believe that it isn't fair to let one child complete a map while another writes an essay. However, it is crucial to understand that a wide variety of methods are acceptable to demonstrate a student's knowledge. It is only necessary for them to do the same thing to demonstrate this knowledge if the activity *is* the assessment. This means that unless you are assessing a student's ability to write an essay, an essay is only one of many ways to evaluate what the student has learned. This realization, above all else, changed most of my beliefs about teaching and learning. Here are some of the choice boards I've used for teaching vocabulary, as well as both fiction and non-fiction.

Vocabulary Choice Board

The first choice board I ever created myself was to review vocabulary, and I still use it now.

Figure 1.1 FMS Vocabulary Board

Freedom   **M**iddle   **S**chool

Find other words with the same prefix, suffix, or root words as the vocabulary words for this week. You should have a prefix, suffix, and root for EACH vocabulary word.	Create a picture card for each word. On one side, write the word and definition. On the other side, create a picture of the word. You may draw, color, paint, make a collage, etc.	Use each word in a sentence about the novel we are currently reading. Try to imitate the author's style of writing when possible.
Make a mini-thesaurus by listing the vocabulary words in alphabetical order, then provide two synonyms for each word.	Create a media mash up of images that represent each word. Use at least two examples for each word.	Create a short story using all the vocabulary words for this week. Be creative!
Find two antonyms for each vocab word. Then, write a sentence using the word and one of the antonyms.	Create an artistic representation of each word. Feel free to improvise.	Write sentences with each word using figurative language.

This is your FMS vocabulary board. For this choice board, you need to **pick one activity from each column** (one F, one M, and one S). This should give you a nice balance of word study, artistic expression, and writing. We will be using these tools to review together.

Some people use their school initials or their own. The appeal of the choice board for teaching vocabulary should be obvious. Drill and kill instruction can be very tedious for both teachers and students, not to mention only useful for the short term. Yet, it often feels like direct instruction is the only way to go—after all, the students don't know the words. Other times, I feel like students will never develop vocabulary unless they are avid readers. And, what about those students with huge vocabulary deficits that are primarily a result of zip code? However, choice boards for vocabulary acquisition have made me more optimistic. Now, I approach it as "Word Study" and differentiate instead of looking for a miracle cure.

When I explored the research regarding vocabulary, I found it to be mountainous but also unclear on the success of any single method. The National Reading Panel (NRP) was tasked by Congress in 1997 to study the existing research on reading pedagogy. In 2000, the NRP published its report, yet refrained from recommending a single specific methodology. However, after comprehensive evaluation of hundreds of reading studies (that had been narrowed down from over 100,000), the NRP published these implications for instruction:

1. Vocabulary should be taught both directly and indirectly.
2. Repetition and multiple exposures to vocabulary items are important.
3. Learning in rich contexts is valuable for vocabulary learning.
4. Vocabulary tasks should be restructured when necessary.
5. Vocabulary learning should entail active engagement in learning task.
6. Computer technology can be used to help teach vocabulary.
7. Vocabulary can be acquired through incidental learning.
8. How vocabulary is assessed and evaluated can have differential effects on instruction.
9. Dependence on a single vocabulary instruction method will not result in optimal learning.

Choice boards provide opportunities for multiple exposures to words, opportunities for active engagement, and direct and indirect vocabulary instruction, while incorporating variety and repetition. An additional benefit of this choice board is that students can exchange their tasks to study. I love the conversation that happens when a student is explaining his metacognitive process with another student and they create yet another access point to retrieve the words.

CCSS.ELA-Literacy.RH.6–8.4

Determine the meaning of words and phrases as they are used in a text, including vocabulary specific to domains related to history/social studies.

CCSS.ELA-Literacy.L.8.4.a

Use context (e.g., the overall meaning of a sentence or paragraph; a word's position or function in a sentence) as a clue to the meaning of a word or phrase.

CCSS.ELA-Literacy.L.8.4.b

Use common, grade-appropriate Greek or Latin affixes and roots as clues to the meaning of a word (e.g., *precede, recede, secede*).

CCSS.ELA-Literacy.L.8.5

Demonstrate understanding of figurative language, word relationships, and nuances in word meanings.

CCSS.ELA-Literacy.L.8.5.b

Use the relationship between particular words to better understand each of the words.

CCSS.ELA-Literacy.L.8.5.c

Distinguish among the connotations (associations) of words with similar denotations (definitions) (e.g., *bullheaded, willful, firm, persistent, resolute*).

Understanding Characters Choice Board

This choice board takes character study beyond simple discussions centered on a list of character traits. One of the goals I have for my students, because ultimately I am still that literature-loving free spirit who wants to talk about books, is to have authentic conversations about what authors actually do to pull at our heartstrings or cause us to talk back to the characters in anger. The Common Core State Standards require students to think about the author's craft and structure in ways that prior standards did not. This choice board helps students and teachers approach the text in a meaningful and challenging way, while also allowing for choice.

6 ◆ Options and Choice

Figure 1.2 Understanding Characters

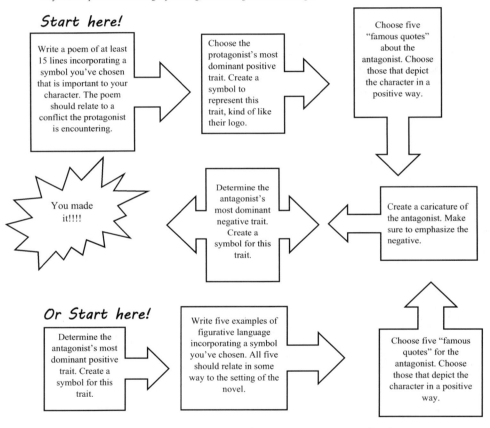

*You may start at the top or the bottom, but you will do a **total of 5 activities**, either direction you choose. When you've completed all tasks, print two copies to share with your classmates.*

CCSS.ELA-Literacy.RL.8.2
Determine a theme or central idea of a text and analyze its development over the course of the text, including its relationship to the

characters, setting, and plot; provide an objective summary of the text.

CCSS.ELA-Literacy.RL.8.3

Analyze how particular lines of dialogue or incidents in a story or drama propel the action, reveal aspects of a character, or provoke a decision.

Fiction Choice Board

This choice board is primarily a comprehension check tool after completing a novel. It can be used for whole group novels or independent reading.

Figure 1.3 Fiction Choice Board

Choose a Plot Task	Choose a Setting Task	Choose a Character Task
✓ Create a timeline of ten major events in the story. ✓ Write a one- to two-page essay explaining the dominant conflict and how it propels the action. ✓ Create a movie poster depicting what you consider to be the climax. ✓ Create a prologue of a page or two. ✓ Create an epilogue of a page or two. ✓ Film a pivotal scene. After you are done, be sure to explain why you made this choice. ✓ Write the music score and/or perform it for a chapter of the book. ✓ Write a letter to the author arguing for a different ending.	✓ Write an explanation of the significance of the setting. ✓ Draw, paint, sketch, etc. a picture of the central setting. ✓ Make a diorama of the setting. ✓ Write the author a letter arguing for a different, better setting. ✓ Write a compare and contrast paragraph about the setting of this novel compared with the last one you read. ✓ Create a Venn diagram of the setting of the book and your own neighborhood. ✓ Make a walking tour video of the setting as you imagine it.	✓ Write a conversation between two characters about the protagonist. ✓ Describe how the protagonist would act at a party. What about a wedding? Or a funeral? ✓ Write a Facebook profile for your character. ✓ Shoot a series of photos that the protagonist would put on Instagram. Give them all a one-line descriptor. ✓ Write your protagonist's horoscope for the last day of the book. ✓ Paint, sculpt, draw, etc. your protagonist.

It tackles "the basics" of plot, setting, and characterization. This is a great example of allowing students to use their talents and passions to demonstrate their knowledge. Students who struggle to comprehend what they read are more likely to continue to dig and re-read when they have an enjoyable and interesting task at hand. On the other hand, those students for whom reading comes easily are able to push themselves beyond a reading comprehension quiz, which can almost become insulting. Additionally, students have summaries available to them literally in the palms of their hands—no longer do students purchase CliffsNotes or go to the library to read summaries, but browse on their smartphones.

One of the benefits I found of using this choice board is that students had more questions than answers, which led to significantly better conversations. It allows students to approach the text from a variety of angles, which is the goal of course, but this is where questions emerge regarding equity. How can a student who chooses to "create a movie poster depicting what you consider to be the climax" and a student who chooses to "write an essay explaining the dominant conflict and how it propels the action" be graded fairly? When asked this question, a teacher must return to the premise that the point is to assess a student's mastery of the standards, not a mastery of the medium. By this I mean that students can "show what they know" in a perfectly "fair" way because the goal is to measure the learning that has occurred and provide meaningful feedback, not check how well they can write an essay—unless, as I mentioned, writing an essay is the skill being assessed.

It is also significant to note that these mini-projects aren't the only ways their understanding will be assessed, but it is important foundationally to create assignments that are accessible to everyone with the built-in potential to push the more skilled students. As students complete the projects, make sure to build in time for them to interact with each other in small groups even if it is as simple as a two-minute "show and tell." This choice board in particular is a great "turn and tell" conversation for students.

As you walk around your room, listen to the future valedictorian asking a shy boy who almost never participates, "What projects did you do? How did you learn to draw anime? Why did you give the protagonist that type of clothing?" Or, you might hear the budding actress convince a shy student to read lines of a skit. These exchanges are noisy, and when I first started orchestrating these moments, I was nervous about their lack of structure, but when students share what they know with others in creative ways, huge walls come tumbling down between different types of students. Those walls are often built upon a teacher's desire to quantify students' *sameness*, missing the fact that the learning actually occurs on the individual level, where the *differences* occur.

> **CCSS.ELA-Literacy.W.8.3**
>
> Write narratives to develop real or imagined experiences or events using effective technique, relevant descriptive details, and well-structured event sequences.
>
> **CCSS.ELA-Literacy.W.8.3.a**
>
> Engage and orient the reader by establishing a context and point of view and introducing a narrator and/or characters; organize an event sequence that unfolds naturally and logically.
>
> **CCSS.ELA-Literacy.W.8.3.b**
>
> Use narrative techniques, such as dialogue, pacing, description, and reflection, to develop experiences, events, and/or characters.

Bloom's Tic-Tac-Toe Choice Board

When reading non-fiction, it is easy to fall into the trap of handing out reading comprehension worksheets. Though brief comprehension checks have their place, students aren't truly engaged when "hunt and find" is the goal. I once caught a student copying another student's answers to a social studies worksheet during lunch. When confronted, he genuinely didn't see the problem. His answer is a great reminder of how students feel about that type of assignment, "She just copied the answers from the book. They were all in order. I didn't have my book, so I just copied what she copied." This choice board engages students, and takes the cognitive load to a completely different level.

> **CCSS.ELA-Literacy.RI.8.2**
>
> Determine a central idea of a text and analyze its development over the course of the text, including its relationship to supporting ideas; provide an objective summary of the text.
>
> **CCSS.ELA-Literacy.RI.8.3**
>
> Analyze how a text makes connections among and distinctions between individuals, ideas, or events (e.g., through comparisons, analogies, or categories).

Bloom's Tic Tac Toe board is also a great social studies tool as well.

Figure 1.4 Bloom's Tic Tac Toe

KNOWLEDGE Collect ten facts or ideas and organize them in a logical way.	APPLICATION Draw a diagram or map of an important topic from your reading.	EVALUATION Judge two different viewpoints about the topic. Write about each.
EVALUATION Forecast how this topic will change/grow/evolve in the next five years. Then, ten years.	Free Choice: Choose one of these activities and use innovation to improve it. Then, do it!	APPLICATION Demonstrate something about your topic to "show what you know."
UNDERSTANDING Create a twenty-question m/c test, w/answers included.	KNOWLEDGE Draw a timeline of at least seven significant events.	SYNTHESIS Teach a lesson about your topic to the class. Include one visual aid.

When you have completed your research, complete three activities for a tic-tac-toe. You should choose the activities that most make sense for the topic you studied.

After assigning a reading about immigration, imagine how students will respond to these higher order thinking activities. Students won't feel as if they can simply copy the answers because they are able to create, demonstrate, predict, diagram, map, or infer. Some may think that students will resist the extra work associated with a choice board like this, but I have witnessed time and time again that assigning students quality opportunities to "show what you know" yields a greater desire to complete the work. The boy I mentioned on the previous page, the one who only "copied what was copied," would be challenged, not bored, by rote learning.

> **CCSS.ELA-Literacy.RH.6–8.2**
> Determine the central ideas or information of a primary or secondary source; provide an accurate summary of the source distinct from prior knowledge or opinions.

> **CCSS.ELA-Literacy.RH.6–8.7**
>
> Integrate visual information (e.g., in charts, graphs, photographs, videos, or maps) with other information in print and digital texts.
>
> **CCSS.ELA-Literacy.WHST.6–8.7**
>
> Conduct short research projects to answer a question (including a self-generated question), drawing on several sources and generating additional related, focused questions that allow for multiple avenues of exploration.

Science teachers may also use the Bloom's Tic Tac Toe board to reinforce literacy skills in their classes. One of the key shifts in thinking in recent years has been that literacy is a cross-curricular endeavor, not something that happens for forty minutes in an ELA class. After assigning a reading about environmental pollution, this choice board would yield some really interesting perspectives. Instead of measuring how well students heard the material, or their reading comprehension, or their ability to scan for the correct answers, you'd know how well a student is understanding the concepts and applying his/her own thinking.

> **CCSS.ELA-Literacy.RST.6–8.7**
>
> Integrate quantitative or technical information expressed in words in a text with a version of that information expressed visually (e.g., in a flowchart, diagram, model, graph, or table).
>
> **CCSS.ELA-Literacy.RST.6–8.8**
>
> Distinguish among facts, reasoned judgment based on research findings, and speculation in a text.

21st-Century Skills Choice Board

In an American Association of School Administrators (AASA) interview with Tom Friedman, author of *The World is Flat*, Daniel Pink, a prolific writer in his own right, summarizes what he thinks the new direction of education should be. Pink says, "It's the combination of the left brain and the right brain. Left-brain thinking—rule-based, linear, SAT-style thinking—used to be enough. Now right-brain thinking—artistry, empathy, narrative, synthesis—is the big differentiator." As their conversation continues, Pink describes the process as "mashing up," essentially putting two things together that don't naturally fit, and says it will be a required skill in a technology-flattened world. The 21st century, with its instant access to information, needs more than what Friedman calls "sifters" and "sorters," but instead, future generations must embrace connections. He never downplays the role of the "sifters" and "sorters," but he also knows that in a world where rote skills are easy to come by, success will be measured by something else. He explains, "So the school, the state, the country that empowers, nurtures, enables imagination among its students and citizens, that's who's going to be the winner" (p. 3).

The 21st-century choice board focuses on the four roles that students need to embrace in order to shape the next century: critical thinker, communicator, collaborator, and creator.

Figure 1.5 21st-Century Skills in Action Research

After you have completed your research, choose a task from each column to demonstrate your mastery of 21st-century skills. Not all tasks are easily transferrable to all topics, so choose what best demonstrates your skills and knowledge. You will hand in four tasks total, each worth one-quarter of your project grade.

NEA P21 Standards:

Analyze how parts of a whole interact with each other to produce overall outcomes in complex systems
Solve different kinds of unfamiliar problems in both conventional and innovative ways

Critical Thinker	Communicator	Collaborator	Creator
Make a new rule for society based on the information you read. Why is this rule needed? What impact will it have? Are there unintended consequences?	Record a public service announcement about this topic. Narrow down your message to a thirty-second sound bite. Consider the tone you want to use (angry, fearful, excited, nervous, etc.) and explain why that tone will best deliver your message.	With two other people, collaborate to create a visual representation of the information you read. You may work on this in person or digitally. Be prepared to explain how you arrived at this visual.	Design a logo for this topic. Be ready to explain the choices you make. Consider size, color, and the symbolism behind what you choose. For example, if you incorporate a dove into your logo, you need to explain why peace is a part of your logo.

Options and Choice ◆ 13

Critical Thinker	Communicator	Collaborator	Creator
Based on what you have learned, what are the ten most important jobs for the future? Explain the primary responsibilities for each job, as well as what type of education is needed.	Use an online survey creator (such as Survey Monkey) to create a ten-question survey to gather the opinions of your peers about a topic you choose from your research. Use at least three different question types. Compile the results into a chart and write an explanation.	Find two experts in the field and write an email about your findings. Ask if they'd like to participate in an email interview. Make a transcript. After you've printed out the transcript, annotate the conversation.	Become a photojournalist for the day. Take a series of at least fifteen pictures related to your topic. Determine a way to share with the class (PowerPoint, Prezi, Haiku Deck, Google Slides, or an actual storyboard). For each photo, write a descriptive caption.
If you were to teach a class on this topic, what would be the best way for students to learn the material? Devise an outline of the main ideas the class would need to address. Who would this class appeal to the most?	Research who your legislators are and write to them.		
Think about an aspect of the issue you studied that you think the government should be involved in/or know about. Be sure to be specific about the reasons you believe s/he should be aware. Map out a plan to provide to improve or solve the situation.	Design a simple machine that would impact this topic in some way. For example, if you were studying conservation, design a rainwater collection contraption. Does this machine already exist? Check for a patent at http://www.uspto.gov.	Design an experiment that would be useful to those studying this topic. The experiment should attempt to prove a hypothesis you make. Record yourself doing the experiment, and explain the steps you are taking. Don't forget to use sequencing words like First, Next, Additionally, Then, Finally, and Last.	

(continued on the next page)

Figure 1.5 Continued

Critical Thinker	Communicator	Collaborator	Creator
If you were to put a dollar value on this topic and how important it is to the world, what would it cost? How do you arrive at that number? Provide a written explanation.	Make a commercial about some aspect of your topic. It may be an advertisement, informational, or political in nature. What message are you trying to convey? Who is your intended audience? Is there anyone who would be offended? Why? Include music to set the tone.	Design a webpage about your topic. Find several classmates to contribute their talents: design, copywriting, music, technology, etc. Make sure that you provide an "About Us" page to introduce your collaborators. Send me the link.	Create a soundtrack of music that would help inform the public about your topic. Consider the tone, as well as the meaning of the lyrics. Include the lyrics to each song and your annotations. Take notice of how the writer uses figurative language, imagery, and repetition (particularly in the refrain/chorus).

Identify and ask significant questions that *clarify* various points of view and lead to better solutions.
Articulate thoughts and ideas effectively using oral, written, and nonverbal communication skills in a variety of forms.
Elaborate, *refine*, *analyze*, and *evaluate* original ideas to improve and maximize creative effort.

Students are required to complete one task from each column, simulating the confluence of thinking that will be required to be successful in their future. This choice board is easily applied across the curriculum.

For example, the Centers for Disease Control and Prevention has described an effective approach to teaching health curriculum this way:

> Learning experiences correspond with students' cognitive and emotional development, help them personalize information, and maintain their interest and motivation while accommodating diverse capabilities and learning styles. Instructional strategies and learning experiences include methods for
>
> a. Addressing key health-related concepts.
> b. Encouraging creative expression.
> c. Sharing personal thoughts, feelings, and opinions.
> d. Thoughtfully considering new arguments.
> e. Developing critical thinking skills.
> (Centers for Disease Control and Prevention, 2013)

Given these guidelines, this choice board is an excellent tool to personalize information. After studying the importance of healthy lifestyle choices, the projects could range from a public service announcement about the importance of sleep, to letters to legislators asking for support in banning e-cigarettes from public places, to a photo essay of negative messaging directed at students in the media.

Menus for Added Direction

As much as I like choice boards, I'm the kind of teacher who likes to have everything in writing, particularly examples and instructions. With 130 students, I've long since realized that saying, "Read the instructions in the menu" is far easier than re-explaining to the whole group. It is also helpful for parents to have the particulars all in one place. A menu, like the ones you use in a restaurant, simply allows the teacher more space for directions.

Let's say you are in the mood for a burger. Would you like to go to a restaurant with only one choice, or would you rather have the choices afforded you at a restaurant whose menu overflows with exciting possibilities? No matter how amazing the single burger actually is, most of us would opt for at least the opportunity to choose, even if you always pick the same choice! As it turns out, when students are given choices, they are more likely to be engaged, push themselves to their full potential, and enjoy the experience.

There are several ways to use these menus. For example, in our "real life" outside of school, when we go to a restaurant, we give our children choices from the menu. We narrow down the scope for the youngest children because too many possibilities are overwhelming. We might say, "You may have either macaroni and cheese OR you may have a hot dog." It is your prerogative as the instructor to use these menus in the same way. If you know that Sue is a slow reader, you might narrow her choices to A, C, or F. She'll still have choices, but you won't allow her to "order" something she couldn't finish. Or, just as your own children are given more choices when they are ready, you may do the same with your students, allowing them the full range of options.

You'll notice that there are almost always "traditional" choices among the more progressive ones. It is important to note how the choices are arranged. The least complicated, lower level assignments are always listed first. For example, an "A" choice is usually appropriate for a struggling student, while an "E" choice is appropriate for an advanced student. The "D," "E," and "F" choices involve higher order thinking skills, as defined by the revised Bloom's taxonomy. I've used these menus for years, several in an inclusion classroom. Not once has anyone noticed this "secret" way to differentiate. This is not to say that a struggling student can't do an "E" activity, or an advanced one an "A" activity, but you have a greater handle on what they will need as support, simply from the choice that is made.

The added benefit for the teacher is that students are working on assignments that interest them, creating grading for you that is enjoyable and allowing you to get to know your students while avoiding "more of the same." I've included rubrics for each assignment as well, so grading becomes holistic and offers feedback quickly. As you use these activities, I am sure that you'll find a greater sense of inclusiveness, as well as the pride that comes with giving students true opportunities for accomplishment instead of expecting cookie cutter compliance.

As you consider these menus and rubrics, take note of the "kid friendly" language used throughout. It may be our responsibility to meet standards and address skills and deficits, but it is also our job to inspire students, and assignments and rubrics written in adult jargon will never do that. There's a time and place for standardized language, but these rubrics aim to give students feedback that will both inform and encourage.

I'm always searching for new rubric models, and I cringe when I see some of the recent standards-based rubrics that call students' work "limited" or "simple." As for me, I can't reconcile talking about the importance of a growth mindset, yet describing a student's work that way. It is also my policy to allow students to revise any project or presentation. When students make that second (or even third) attempt, and the work is so much better, I know that the lighter hand in assessment language has perhaps been less an "honest" view of the child's work, but garnered the result that is best for the child: authentic learning in a safe and supportive environment.

Menu for Class Novels

The menu for class novels is easiest to implement because you are still at the helm, steering the ship.

Figure 1.6 Menu for Class Novels

As we read this novel together, I'd like you to choose three menu items to complete or one "platter." You'll notice that the "platter" options are bigger and require more work. The novel has been "Chunked" into three sections, as follows:

Chunk 1: chapter ____ to chapter ____
Chunk 2: chapter ____ to chapter ____
Chunk 3: chapter ____ to the end

You must complete *one* menu item *per Chunk*. You may complete the same menu item for each Chunk, if you are one of those people who always orders the same thing! If you choose the "platter" option, you won't need to do a task for each Chunk, but instead hand in your "platter" option at the end of Chunk 3.

Choice A) After reading a Chunk, create a ten question multiple choice quiz. Each question should have four answers. One must be the **distracter (an answer that is VERY nearly the correct one)**. At least three questions should refer to literary terms. Two questions should address the theme. You will need to provide an answer key. Your answer key needs to include the answer, the page or pages you used to formulate the question, and a brief explanation of your wrong answers. If I choose to use your quiz, you will receive an extra quiz grade—plus, you wouldn't have to take the quiz!

> **CCSS.ELA-Literacy.RL.8.2**
> Determine a theme or central idea of a text and analyze its development over the course of the text, including its relationship to the characters, setting, and plot; provide an objective summary of the text.

Choice B) Before reading a Chunk, interview a classmate about what s/he thinks will happen next. You may do this on camera or on paper. You'll need four or five questions. Be sure to make them "thick" questions—questions that require deep thoughts, not a yes or no answer. For example, a ho-hum question might be "Do you think *Divergent* is a good book?" The answer is either yes or no, depending on what you think. A "thick" question might be "How do you think Tris might represent the average teenager?" This requires you to have a conversation with multiple possible answers.

> **CCSS.ELA-Literacy.RL.8.3**
> Analyze how particular lines of dialogue or incidents in a story or drama propel the action, reveal aspects of a character, or provoke a decision.

Choice C) Before reading a Chunk, **skim** and **scan** the text. (**Skim means to look over without reading, letting your mind jump from part to part. Scan means to look over the text, reading some lines**.) Choose five words that you don't know. Create a dictionary entry for the words. Write your dictionary entry on a 3 × 5 card in marker and give them to me to place on our word wall. A dictionary entry has the following components: the word, the part of speech, at least one definition, and a sentence using the word. When writing the sentence for the word, use the sentence from the novel. Here is an example:

> **Noncommittal**: adjective; not involving or showing commitment to a particular opinion, view, or course of action. *When asked where he was going, Jed was very noncommittal.*

CCSS.ELA-Literacy.L.8.4.c
Consult general and specialized reference materials (e.g., dictionaries, glossaries, thesauruses), both print and digital, to find the pronunciation of a word or determine or clarify its precise meaning or its part of speech.

CCSS.ELA-Literacy.L.8.4.d
Verify the preliminary determination of the meaning of a word or phrase (e.g., by checking the inferred meaning in context or in a dictionary).

Choice D) After reading a Chunk, choose an object from that part of the novel and do an artistic representation of it. You may do a sculpture, take a picture, do a collage, knit it, sew it, weave it, draw it, paint it, and so forth. Whatever you do artistically, the only requirement is to incorporate five symbols or themes from the Chunk associated with it. For example, if you were using the story of Cinderella, you might create a paper-sculptured pumpkin. For the stem, you might use crumbled brown bags. On the stem, you might write the words: CINDERELLA, MIDNIGHT, MICE, PRINCE, FAIRY GODMOTHER. Write a paragraph about each of the symbols or themes you chose, describing the impact it has on the story (total of five paragraphs).

CCSS.ELA-Literacy.RL.8.9
Analyze how a modern work of fiction draws on themes, patterns of events, or character types from myths, traditional stories, or religious works such as the Bible, including describing how the material is rendered new.

Choice E) After reading a Chunk, you will need to create a public service announcement (PSA) about what happened. PSAs are to help society understand information. An example of a PSA might be a campaign to stop people from leaving pets in their cars. Your PSA might be about a character's actions. For example, if your protagonist is ignoring his schoolwork to focus on football, your PSA might be about the importance of grades and the small chance of becoming a professional athlete.

CCSS.ELA-Literacy.SL.8.5
Integrate multimedia and visual displays into presentations to clarify information, strengthen claims and evidence, and add interest.

Platter A) Create a test on the novel. It should include ten multiple choice questions regarding the *plot* (*what happened*). Make sure each question has a *distracter* (*an answer that is VERY nearly the correct one*). Create three short answer questions that could be answered in about a paragraph. You should focus on *characterization* (*how the author makes the characters real*). After you have typed up the test, print a clean copy. Then, print another copy with the answers circled for the multiple choice and the short answer questions answered with what you consider to be exemplary answers. If I decide to use your test, you don't have to take it!

> **CCSS.ELA-Literacy.RL.8.2**
> Determine a theme or central idea of a text and analyze its development over the course of the text, including its relationship to the characters, setting, and plot; provide an objective summary of the text.
>
> **CCSS.ELA-Literacy.RL.8.3**
> Analyze how particular lines of dialogue or incidents in a story or drama propel the action, reveal aspects of a character, or provoke a decision.

Platter B) Create a talk show. You'll need to gather the help of your talented friends. One person will need to be the host of the show. The other person will need to be the author of the novel. The person who is the author will need to answer at least five substantial questions about his/her choices as an author.

If you were interviewing Suzanne Collins, the author of *The Hunger Games*, you might ask, "Why do you create the Capitol as so over-the top glamorous and outrageous?" or "What were you trying to say about video games since it is the Gamemakers who create the absolute worst parts of the Hunger Games?" The person who plays the author needs to have really detailed answers, supported by the book itself. For example,

> Well, I wanted there to be a stark contrast between District 12 and the lavish world of the Capitol, as well as make the reader see the results of greed. As for the videogames aspect, I like my readers to relate to the story, and so many students are gamers. But, I'm also hoping that everyone realizes the power they have over everyone else.

You may perform the skit for the class or videotape it, and I'll show it. Have fun with this!

> **CCSS.ELA-Literacy.SL.8.4**
> Present claims and findings, emphasizing salient points in a focused, coherent manner with relevant evidence, sound valid reasoning, and well-chosen details; use appropriate eye contact, adequate volume, and clear pronunciation.
>
> **CCSS.ELA-Literacy.SL.8.5**
> Integrate multimedia and visual displays into presentations to clarify information, strengthen claims and evidence, and add interest.

Platter C) Research a topic from the novel that interests you. For example, if you read James Dashner's *Maze Runner*, you might research how codes have been used throughout history. Prepare a presentation of eight to ten minutes for the class. You may use PowerPoint, posters, or do a speech. You will need to hand in a brief (two pages or so) report of your research with a Works Cited page.) You will need to use *parenthetical citations of direct quotes. Parenthetical citations list the page where you found the information as it corresponds to the Works Cited page. Direct quotes are words directly copied from the text.* Here are some examples:

Website
According to *teenhealth.com*, "Teenagers who grow up in their grandparents' home frequently rebel" (3).

Database
The database, *Myths and Legends Online Database*, "King Arthur is an example of a meek vs. the mighty theme" (4).

Book
In the novel, *Freak the Mighty*, Rodman Philbrick created Grim and Gram who allow Max to live "in the DownUnder," the basement of their house (39).

> **CCSS.ELA-Literacy.W.8.7**
> Conduct short research projects to answer a question (including a self-generated question), drawing on several sources and generating additional related, focused questions that allow for multiple avenues of exploration.
>
> **CCSS.ELA-Literacy.W.8.8**
> Gather relevant information from multiple print and digital sources, using search terms effectively; assess the credibility and accuracy of each source; and quote or paraphrase the data and conclusions of others while avoiding plagiarism and following a standard format for citation.

You'll help students "chunk" the novel, set deadlines, and organize their thinking going into the project. Additionally, as you formatively assess throughout the novel, you'll know who might need a helping hand and who is ready to go it alone. This type of control over the big picture is what made implementing this menu easy.

You'll also notice the bolded words on the menu. These are words that I teach, and I am using the menu to reinforce the vocabulary. Some of the words are simply vocabulary that may be difficult, like "noncommittal." Other words are testing words—"distracter" and "skim and scan." As a layer of vocabulary instruction, embedding the vocabulary is an excellent way to give students a look at the words in another context. Additionally, students are generally very emotionally connected to their projects, so another type of linking to the vocabulary can never hurt.

Figure 1.7 Rubric for Class Novel Projects

NICE WORK!!!	ALMOST THERE!!!	KEEP WORKING!!!	NEEDS WORK!!!
Your project shows that you truly understood the task at hand and sought to show your knowledge in "thick" ways with substantial (deep) questions and answers. You added greatly to our class. /70	Your project shows that you understood the task at hand and you "kinda" tried to show your ideas; however, your answers are not as substantial (deep) as they should be. I know you've got more to give! /60	Your project shows that you might not understand all parts of the task at hand. You may have needed to ask some questions as you prepared. Your answers show some problems with your thinking. /50	Your project shows that you didn't read the book or understand some key element. You seemed to be struggling and may have just been wrong about something. Your answers aren't ready to share yet. See me if you need some help. /40
Correct grammar and mechanics in all written components. This provides an exemplar for the class. Seek to help others when they need it. You are a grammar guru! /20	Mostly correct grammar and mechanics in all written components. Our class could help with the small problems. Talk to a grammar guru next time to edit with you. /15	The grammar and mechanics of the written components are draft quality. This means that the errors you make are not acceptable for a polished piece. You need some help from our expert editors. /10	The grammar and mechanics are not acceptable for the assignment. You may have used bullets or written phrases. You struggled to put what was in your head on to the page. This is a first draft. /5
Creativity and initiative are evident in the final product. You rocked this assignment, and I will show you off any chance I get! Innovative and interesting. /10	Creativity and initiative are evident, but you may need a little more of one or the other! I'm feeling it, but I think you could do more. Push past your worries and take a risk. /7	Creativity and initiative aren't clear. Help me see what you were thinking! You may have used a template or did this exactly like you did last time. Tap the left brain! /5	Creativity and initiative are lacking. I am not able to see what you are thinking. Your final product is not acceptable. Let's brainstorm so we can get this thing conquered! We need to find your inspiration! /3

Notes for me (tell me what I should be noticing!):

My comments to you (I'll tell you what stood out!):

As mentioned earlier, the choices are organized from least complicated, knowledge-based questions (A, B, and C) to higher order tasks (D and E). Students frequently mistake the first options as the most difficult because they are more traditional, and they think that the creative questions must be easier. This is a perfect opportunity to have overt conversations about Bloom's taxonomy or left and right brain tasks. It is always my goal to emphasize that all the tasks are valuable, and I treat them all equally in my feedback.

The platter options are designed for the overachievers in your class. They are more time-consuming and are great enrichment opportunities for those students who inevitably read ahead. Notice, though, that the tasks are not necessarily *more* work, but a deeper kind of work. These tasks involve multiple modalities, and create opportunities for students who already know the content to stretch themselves and stay engaged. This generates opportunities to use linguistic, visual, and audio modes to conceptualize and create meaning. The tasks involve skills that I may not have taught yet, so there is instruction embedded in the task via the examples and models. I've long been disturbed that a one-size-fits-all approach to student learning shortchanges the exceptionalities—Special Education and gifted students. When possible, I tailor these platter options to students I have in my class. For instance, Platter B was designed explicitly to challenge several of my students who were high achievers, but also involved in drama. Even within the differentiated assignments, I always try to zero in on the particular facts I have about students to tap into their passions, as this increases student engagement and retention of the learning.

Menu for Independent Reading

Independent reading assignments frequently are the catalyst for some of the most dreadful, boring, and mindless copying activities. This menu strives to alleviate the boredom, while also ensuring that students read their independent reading novel.

Choice A and B, again, are more traditional, but in this case very important scaffolding for the struggling reader. Choice A is helpful for students who need to keep track of the plot, while Choice B is actually pre-teaching for a language lesson we do later involving register.

Teachers may elect to use the student products of these activities to entice them to make good choices for their next Independent Reading project. For example, I've used the "Letters to the Protagonist" activity as a teaser for the novel, having the students share a few entries with the

Figure 1.8 Independent Reading

To demonstrate your knowledge about the book you've read independently, choose from the menu that follows. Just like a menu at a restaurant, you want to read carefully to understand what you are ordering! Different menu items may have different due dates, so make sure you write it down when I announce them.

Choice A) LETTERS TO THE PROTAGONIST

Due Date: _____

After each chapter, send the *protagonist* (*main character*) a short letter (about a paragraph). Remember, a good paragraph has between five and eight sentences. Keep the letters in the order of the chapters. When you hand in this task, you should have the same number of paragraphs as chapters in your book.

Q and A:

Q: I don't know what to write about!

A: Ask your character questions, respond to something s/he said, discuss another character, discuss the *plot* (*what happens in the story*), discuss the *setting* (*where the story happened*), or tell the character about something in your life that relates to his or her life.

Choice B) FAMOUS QUOTES

Due Date: _____

As you read each chapter, flag (with a sticky note) any *dialogue* (*conversation between characters*) that you think is interesting or significant. At the end of the chapter, find three pieces of dialogue and rewrite it. As you rewrite the dialogue, change the *register* (*the level of formality used in speech*). For example, if the *register* is formal, make it informal, or vice versa.

Example:

(original dialogue in formal *register*)

"Hark! Where art thou commencing from? Come hither!"

(revised dialogue in casual *register*)

"Hey! Where were you? Get over here!"

When you hand in this task, you should have three pieces of dialogue for each chapter. Multiply the number of chapters by three to come up with the number you should have.

Choice C) DRAMATIC MONOLOGUE

Due Date: _____

Choose the most intense moment of the book, possibly the *climax* (*the highest point of action*). Now, write a speech from the *protagonist*'s point of view. This speech should be to the reader (you) describing what it feels like to be in the given situation. For example, the *protagonist* might have been caught lying. The *dramatic monologue* (*speech given by a character, usually in a play*) must be two minutes long, and you need to be ready to deliver it to the class. You don't have to memorize it, but you mustn't read it.

Hint:

Chunk the speech into about six parts. Print them out in HUGE letters so it will be easy to read while you are presenting.

Choice D) CARTOGRAPHER

Due Date: _____

Your job for this task is to be a *cartographer* (*mapmaker*) for the novel you read. You may use the computer or do this by hand. Your map should be beautifully designed and colorful. There should be a *key* (*a list of the symbols you used on the map and what those symbols stand for*) with at least seven fascinating places your character visited. You will most likely need to use your imagination to create the map. Pay close attention to details about the *setting* (*where the story happens*). Your map will be showcased in our room, so make sure it is neat with everything spelled correctly. You will need to write a short paragraph about each of the places your character visited. Remember, even a short paragraph must have at least five sentences.

Choice E) BOOK CRITIC

Due Date: _____

Your task is to be a book *critic* (*someone whose job it is to judge a work based on its merits*). First, you must read several book reviews online. Print out at least three of them. Highlight the *adjectives* (*descriptive words*) that the book critic used. You will likely encounter phrases that are interesting as well and may highlight those.

For example:

"page turner"
"spellbinding"
"a real thriller"
"brilliantly imagined"
"a definite tear-jerker"

After studying the language of the book review, write your own. Make sure that your *critique* (*the piece a critic writes*) does not ruin the ending. Be sure to include at least two or three of the adjectives or phrases you found in your research of book *critiques*. This piece is likely about one typed page.

---

class. Posting the quotes in both casual and formal register from Choice B is an excellent way to expose students to word study in casual, non-instructional ways. Choice C, the Dramatic Monologue, is a tremendous teaser for the novel as well, often convincing students to choose it for their next Independent Reading book. The map is also a great classroom decoration, showcasing students' talents in an area that may not usually get much attention. Choice E, the Book Critic, is another "hook" to help readers, particularly those who struggle, pick an appropriate book. The rubric allows the teacher to evaluate holistically.

Figure 1.9 Independent Reading Project Rubric

	The Conventions *(This is the part of the project where you follow the directions of the project and the rules of the English language)*	**The Ideas** *(This is the part where you had to think, analyze, explain, make connections, etc.)*	**The Product** *(This is the part you actually hand in)*
4	Perfect attention to quality. Demonstrates excellent sentence structure, grammar, spelling, and punctuation. The quantity of writing matches the task.	Perfect attention to the task at hand. The project demonstrates complex thinking, and there are multiple, detailed references, allusions, or quotes from the text.	Book title, author, and your name are prominently displayed. It looks AWESOME! It is colorful, neat, typed, and organized. This is a model of pride in your work.
3	Good attention to quality. Demonstrates good sentence structure, grammar, spelling, and punctuation (with three or fewer minor errors). The quantity is pretty adequate for the task.	Good attention to the task at hand. The project demonstrates accurate thinking, and there are multiple, detailed references, allusions, or quotes, although the choices may not be the most appropriate.	Book title, author, and your name are on the project, but may be harder to find. It looks GREAT! It may not be as colorful, neat, or organized as expected. It may be handwritten. This is a good job, but I know you can do better.
2	Attention to quality is lacking. Demonstrates repetitive sentence structure or problems forming complete sentences. More than four different grammar and spelling errors. The quantity is not appropriate for the task.	Attention to the task at hand is lacking, or the project demonstrates a lack of familiarity with the book. The projects contains errors in thinking, and there are not multiple, detailed references, allusions, or quotes.	Book title, author, and your name may not be easy to find. It looks OK. It may not be as colorful, neat, or organized as expected. It may be handwritten. It is a WORK IN PROGRESS because it isn't quite done or is missing something.
1	Quality is lacking. May be bullet points, one long sentence, incoherent, or impossible to read.	Attention is seriously lacking. The project does not refer to the text in references, allusions, or quotes.	Book title, author, and your name may be missing. It looks RUSHED. It is not colorful, neat, or organized. It is missing several parts.

Menu for Presentations

Project based learning is a big aspect of my class, and a crucial component is presenting before an authentic audience. Before we dig into a full-fledged, "burning question" based project, I like students to have opportunities to present that are lower key. This is the menu I offer during the first quarter, as we are getting to know one another and need to gain confidence in our skills.

Figure 1.10 Presentation Menu Options

Now that we have finished writing, it is time to share our knowledge with our learning community—each other! As always, I think it is super important that you share in teaching what you have learned because it is not until you share that your knowledge is tested. Choose a presentation option from the menu below.

Option A) PowerPoint Presentation
Create a presentation of between five and ten slides. Your presentation should include all aspects of the writing. Each idea should be represented in some way. Remember, you are not reading from the slides, but using them as talking points.

> **CCSS.ELA-Literacy.SL.8.5**
> Integrate multimedia and visual displays into presentations to clarify information, strengthen claims and evidence, and add interest.

Option B) Media Mash Up
Create a "media mash up"—this is a digital collage. It may include photographs of people, places, things, ideas, artwork, websites, quotes, text, and music. It is up to you to represent the work of your writing in a mostly non-linguistic representation. You will need to explain the connections that your "media mash up" is making.

> **CCSS.ELA-Literacy.SL.8.5**
> Integrate multimedia and visual displays into presentations to clarify information, strengthen claims and evidence, and add interest.

Option C) Skit, Talk Show, or Live Event
This option is for my performers. Create a skit, organize a talk show, or stage some other live event. For example, you may choose to write a song and perform it. You are the lead in your own show!

> **CCSS.ELA-Literacy.SL.8.6**
> Adapt speech to a variety of contexts and tasks, demonstrating command of formal English when indicated or appropriate.

Option D) Video
This is essentially Option C, but NOT "before a live audience."

Options and Choice ◆ 27

CCSS.ELA-Literacy.SL.8.6

Adapt speech to a variety of contexts and tasks, demonstrating command of formal English when indicated or appropriate.

Option E) Create and deliver a mini-lesson

Whether you know it or not, you've seen many mini-lessons. When a teacher gives you a five- to seven-minute lesson, that is considered a mini-lesson. It is your job to teach the class something you learned through your writing. You'll need to use exciting methods to reach your audience. This may include handouts, questioning, and so forth.

CCSS.ELA-Literacy.SL.8.5

Integrate multimedia and visual displays into presentations to clarify information, strengthen claims and evidence, and add interest.

Rubric for Presentations

Oscar-Worthy	Opening Night	In Rehearsal
This presentation holds the attention of the audience because it is polished, smooth, and the speaker is enthusiastic. The presenter remembers that the audience needs you to be enthusiastic, organized, and in charge. /50 points	These presenters have star quality too, but may have left some of it at the door. The audience may not follow all parts of the presentation because the presenter might be disorganized, mumble, or might just be too quiet. Rehearse more. /40 points	The presenter is struggling to get the "act" together. Remember that presentations are performance and need rehearsal! The speaker may be inaudible, mumble, or seem miserable. We need to talk about how to improve your skills. /30 points
The details are fabulous. I especially like that the presenter has used details that are specific. Everything is spelled correctly, and the content focuses on the most relevant points. /30 points	The details are good. The presenter may have spelled something incorrectly, added some details that don't "fit," or were too generalized. Next time, practice with a partner to make sure it flows. /20 points	This presentation significantly lacks details. It was probably really short because there was not enough content. We need to know names, places, specifics. The presentation is riddled with mistakes. /10 points
The presentation is clearly creative and inspired and has the mark of the presenter's personality. This presentation is an original. /20 points	The presentation isn't "cookie cutter," but it could have been jazzed up a bit with some original pictures, sounds, or your own touch. /15 points	The presenter didn't use left-brain thinking. Maybe more time was needed. Much of it seems to be cut and pasted. Take some creative risks. /10 points

It also allows students a low-risk entrance into using technology to express themselves. Though we all know they are "screen-addicted," without opportunities to use technology for education on a regular basis, their devices will be relegated to simple portable gaming stations and texting devices.

In addition to the technology component, presentations serve several greater purposes. First, I've found that when students are sharing their authentic projects, there is a new excitement in class that is contagious. When students are excited to see one another "show what they know," learning is occurring for those who are presenting and those in the audience. Another crucial component of educating for the 21st century is to make sure that the Speaking and Listening Standards are not ignored. With other pressing (read: testable) standards in play, Speaking and Listening can be pushed aside, ironically, while they are likely the most authentic 21st-century requirements.

When I think of my classes from years past, it is amazing how I remember them by the projects they shared with me. Recently, I received a Facebook message from Amanda, a student I taught seven or eight years ago. She was catching me up on her life, her switched college majors, and her exciting foray into filmmaking. As she expressed her anticipation about her future, she wrote, "I'm pretty sure I technically wrote my first screenplay in your class for *The Pigman*, actually!" She then went on to say "My middle school experience was not very social, and if it wasn't for the bits of support from my teachers that helped boost my lacking confidence, I'm not really sure how I would have gone after the things I have."

As I've expanded my differentiating over the years, I still look at choice boards and menu options as solid, low-stress, high-outcome ways to reach all students. As I work to differentiate for students, giving options and choice is a first step towards a classroom where lessons aren't taught, but rather, learning experiences offered.

Your Turn

Now that you've read about choice boards and menus, think about how they might work in your own classroom!

- *You can differentiate content, process, or product.* Which will you tinker with first?
- *Fairness will be questioned.* In your own words, how will you explain why students can complete different tasks?

- *21st-century skills change the game.* How will you empower, nurture, and enable imagination in your classroom?
- *Differentiation does not have to be all or nothing.* How will you creatively limit the choices of students who might need more structure?
- *Authentic learning is messy, loud, and chaotic.* What classroom management ideas do you need to implement to manage the learning experiences?

2

Strategic Groupings

Flexibility for Student Engagement

One of the most heated but very quiet debates among teachers is about how we group our students, both in our classrooms and in the way we arrange our schools. It is a controversial topic, and passions run high on both sides, yet there is a significant silence from the field on this in recent years—at least publicly. The contradictory research does little to clarify the question of "best practice." Some say ability grouping "meets students where they are," while others say that "tracking" leads to substandard instruction. Some say that organizing students by talent makes all the sense in the world, while others say that it is a socioeconomic sieve.

As is true with most complex topics, the answer probably lies somewhere in between. I've taught on both sides of the question. As an AP Literature teacher, I was obviously dealing with similar students. For ten of the last fifteen years, however, I've been the regular education ELA teacher on an inclusion team, meaning that I have the entire range of students with the support of Special Education teachers. I've drawn my own conclusions about the effectiveness of both approaches and come to an astonishing realization: A truly differentiated classroom greatly diminishes the "problem" of groupings because it is both heterogeneous *and* homogenous, depending on the needs of the students.

Sneak Peek

This chapter reveals . . .

- *what strategic groupings are and why you should use them*
- *how to gather observational data to help place students appropriately*
- *the power of Fishbowl discussions for student learning*
- *social reading strategies and ways to use them in your classroom*
- *ways to collaborate for all curriculums*
- *how to level tasks by ability and purpose.*

Different Lessons Require Different Arrangements

In a differentiated classroom, the teacher is constantly using formative assessment and observations to cycle students through a variety of arrangements. Simply put, when students *are learning*, staying in a single group would be stifling, just as it would be a huge detriment to stay in a single group if a student *were not learning*. The solution is a rotation of strategic groupings that meet the needs of students at different stages of the learning process. I use strategic groups in my classroom, each emphasizing what is best for students for the particular task at hand—initial exposure, rehearsal, and authentic assessment. A classroom that meets the needs of students is safe, organic, and malleable, a continuous adventure towards self-actualization. If that sounds overwrought, stay tuned for a true story—just like the kind I'm sure you experience in your own classroom—of a student's growth through strategic groupings.

Resource Groups (Initial Introduction and Direct Instruction)

Students are assigned to Resource Groups based on classroom management and the dynamics of that specific group of students. For the first several weeks, I allow students to sit where they wish, and I take notice of successful partnerships, as well as students who probably shouldn't even be in the same room together. I observe moments of compassion, empathy, and collaboration. I'm equally vigilant to notice bullying behavior, condescending attitudes, or uncomfortable students.

This is time-consuming and requires a few weeks of lighter academic activity, but I choose to start my year with trust-building activities that focus on growth mindset, teamwork, and getting to know one another. There are certainly some teachers who breeze through the first day, "lay down the law," and jump into the curriculum content. I was one of those teachers for many years. I felt there was so much to do and so little time, so how could I waste a second? The thing is, a differentiated classroom is not curriculum- or content-centered, but student-centered. If a student feels valued and knows that I am systematically and diligently trying to get to know him/her, there will be more engagement when the learning is academic.

Covert Ways to Plan Your Groups

My favorite activity to bring out a group's true colors is called the Marshmallow Challenge. As students build the tallest freestanding tower from five large marshmallows, twenty small marshmallows, and fifteen toothpicks, it becomes evident who your leaders are, who will sit silently, and who will goof off given the opportunity. I give each group a paper plate (so my desks aren't sticky) and their supplies, then circulate with my notebook, observing. I keep a stockpile of small prizes on hand, but most of the times I make up some "grand prize," like getting to leave class thirty seconds early. I sometimes videotape a group, and I take photos for reference since I might not know students by name yet. I'm honest about my intentions, telling them that I am observing how they work and what kind of group member they are.

Students also do an introductory activity requiring them to speak in front of the class. I have them create a one- to two-minute digital mash up of their favorite things. They share this quick blast of information with the class, and I scribble down insights. It is telling what students will choose to share when they are given such a brief opportunity to represent themselves. I try to glean enough information to make sure that students at Resource Groups have something in common, as well as note talents that emerge. It is useful to notice a student's artistic talent, technological aptitude, or other skills that can translate into success for students.

Granted, this entire process can feel like making seating arrangements for a wedding reception, but most of us have been at the wedding where the seating made us miserable. Ever been seated with a table of old friends who don't include you in the conversation because it is one inside joke after another? Or, a table of complete strangers who have halting conversations because there is nothing in common? Now, imagine being a self-conscious teenager or a timid young child trying to navigate a similar situation, all while trying to learn. These first activities may seem time-consuming, but creating the best learning environment evokes knowledge of students in a way that looking at a roster won't provide.

The reason I take the time to gather this observational data—besides the obvious positive impact on the classroom culture—is that I plan for Resource Groups to stay together for the semester, at least. There are always changes, but I have found that having a "home base" in a constantly changing classroom such as mine is a benefit to everyone. When an activity goes awry, as it inevitably does sometimes, I'm relieved to be able to call a time out and send everyone back to their Resource Groups. Students are more willing to take risks in their other groupings if they feel at home somewhere in the room. These groups, as I mentioned, are heterogeneous, behavior-based, and respectful of students' pre-existing relationships and shared interests. I do not tell students what I am doing or how I'm grouping them in this phase because I don't want to tell them how I am grouping them in other phases when academic ability comes into play. If students ask, I tell them that they will be moved around all the time, so they'll eventually work with everyone, which is true.

When I am introducing new material or beginning a unit, we will begin in these Resource Groups. I need the highest level of compliance in terms of behavior, and from my observations this grouping works best. In the early stages of a unit, I have many "turn and talk" moments, as well as brainstorming sessions. Additionally, this is often the stage when students are taking notes or making learning tools for the unit, both activities that benefit from a level of comfort with each other. Essentially, during the most crucial early stages, students are in a no-risk environment. Carol Tomlinson, the guru of Differentiation with a Capital D, explains the three basic ways researchers have learned that students can differ in how they learn: readiness, interest, and learning profile. Resource Groups address the learning profile of students—factors that can include gender, preferred method of learning, comfort level, and many intangibles that we can only learn from actually knowing the student herself.

For Kaylee Caputo-Davis, a very shy young lady in my afternoon ELA class, the Resource Group was critical in her journey to participation. Kaylee refused to speak in front of the class or participate during her 7th-grade year, fully owning the zeros she received, but never budging. I noticed Kaylee when she came in the room because she kept her head down, even as I stood at the door to greet students. However, during the Marshmallow Challenge and subsequent "get-to-know-you" conversations, Laura Klein, my Special Education partner, noticed that Kaylee C, as we were calling her, seemed comfortable talking with two other students, Amber and Emily. They are bubbly, outgoing overachievers who are, simply put, nice. I jotted it down, and I knew I had the makings of a Resource Group. Kaylee's initial comfort level within her Resource Group paved the way for future success in other groupings.

One of the most engaging activities I use in my class is Fishbowl discussions.

Figure 2.1 Utopia Fishbowl Preparation

***The Giver* Pre-Reading Activity**

Group members:

_____ , _____ , _____ , _____ ,
_____ , _____

Tomorrow you will be doing a Fishbowl on one of the following topics. You and your group should prepare today and tonight. It is a fifteen-point classwork grade using the Fishbowl rubric. This Fishbowl is somewhat different because it asks for your opinions, so make sure you have thought your ideas through. Just because you are answering based on opinion does NOT mean you don't have to use textual evidence.

Each group will need an "opening statement" to let the class know what the question was about and your collective summary.

This Fishbowl will be *organic* (*developing naturally*), so the timing is flexible. We can spare time for a second day, so don't feel rushed.

Remember, take notes on your Fishbowl Notesheet. This is crucial because even though you are only participating in one Fishbowl, you will need to apply your listening skills to gather information from the groups. These five questions are on the final objective test for the novel.

Resource Group #1: What Is a Utopia?

—Define
—Look at our Bill of Rights—is this utopian?
—Is it possible to have a society that all people agree on? Why or why not?
—Think/talk about the quote as it impacts the idea of a utopia:

> When we lose the right to be different, we lose the privilege to be free.
> (Charles Evans Hughes, Address at Faneuil Hall, Boston, Massachusetts, June 17, 1925)

CCSS.ELA-Literacy.RH.6–8.6
Identify aspects of a text that reveal an author's point of view or purpose (e.g., loaded language, inclusion or avoidance of particular facts).

Resource Group #2: Transforming the United States Into a Utopia

—If you were to improve our society/world, what would you change? (examples: poverty, homelessness, etc.)
—How would you go about making those changes?
—What kind of government would work best to create this utopia?
—Think/talk about the quote as it impacts the idea of a utopia:

> For to be free is not merely to cast off one's chains, but to live in a way that respects and enhances the freedom of others.
>
> (Nelson Mandela)

CCSS.ELA-Literacy.SL.8.1.c
Pose questions that connect the ideas of several speakers and respond to others' questions and comments with relevant evidence, observations, and ideas.

Resource Group #3: Bullying and Power

—How would you eliminate bullying? Is that possible?
—What is the relationship between bullying and power?
—Look at the Dignity for All Students Act (DASA). Do a keyword search of the word "DASA." Watch a video about the topic. What do you notice?

CCSS.ELA-Literacy.SL.8.2
Analyze the purpose of information presented in diverse media and formats (e.g., visually, quantitatively, orally) and evaluate the motives (e.g., social, commercial, political) behind its presentation.

Resource Group #4: Connotations and Conclusions

—Remember that a connotation is the feelings associated with a word and denotation is the dictionary definition. For this discussion, you'll be talking about both.
—Look at this list of words: infraction, interdependence, relinquish, infringe, unanimous.

  Determine their denotation.
  What connotation does each word have?
  What conclusions can we draw about this book, based on these words?

—The precise meaning of words is very important in this book. Why might that matter? (think about our conversation about good vs. stupendous, tiny vs. microscopic).

CCSS.ELA-Literacy.L.8.5.c
Distinguish among the connotations (associations) of words with similar denotations (definitions) (e.g., *bullheaded, willful, firm, persistent, resolute*).

Resource Group #5: Real Utopias

—Throughout history, societies have tried to form utopias. Research one that was pre-1900 and another that was post-1900. Discuss with each other your findings and identify two similarities and two differences.

> **CCSS.ELA-Literacy.CCRA.W.7**
> Conduct short as well as more sustained research projects based on focused questions, demonstrating understanding of the subject under investigation.

The room is arranged in a horseshoe or circle—whatever works best for your space. Inside, set up a table with five or six spots for students. The students in the middle are the "fish," and the observers on the outside are looking at and listening to the fish, who are having a discussion.

To prepare for this discussion, which will be used to assess students' understanding of both the questions and their ability to converse, students begin in their Resource Groups. The first step is to give the Resource Groups all of the questions that could be discussed later in the Fishbowl. I overtly explain what is being asked in each question, give tips, and review what I'll be assessing when they do their Fishbowl a few days later.

Figure 2.2 Fishbowl Discussion Rubric

	Developing (1 or 2 points)	**Meets Standard (3, 4, 5 points)**	**Above Standard (5 points +++)**
Prepare and "Show What You Know" **CCSS.ELA-Literacy. SL.8.1.a** Come to discussions prepared, having read or researched material under study; explicitly draw on that preparation by referring to evidence on the topic, text, or issue to probe and reflect on ideas under discussion. /5	You may not have taken proper notes during the preparation period. It seems like you aren't sure of "what you know" and need more time to think or reread. You may not share enough for me to determine what you know.	You are prepared, and use the notes you have created to add to the conversation. You are able to contribute to what is being said with evidence AND raise questions of your own. It is clear that you know that topic and contribute appropriately.	You are a leader within the conversation, using evidence that you have prepared to make interesting points, draw others into the conversation, and are able to reflect on ideas presented to point out connections or misconceptions.

	Developing **(1 or 2 points)**	**Meets Standard** **(3, 4, 5 points)**	**Above Standard** **(5 points +++)**
Loud and clear **CCSS.ELA-Literacy. SL.8.4** Present claims and findings, emphasizing salient points in a focused, coherent manner with relevant evidence, sound valid reasoning, and well-chosen details; use appropriate eye contact, adequate volume, and clear pronunciation. /5	You mumble, cover your mouth, or simply don't speak loud enough for people outside of the Fishbowl to hear you. Sometimes people you are talking to can't hear you. You are not making eye contact with the group members.	You are heard and understood by everyone outside the Fishbowl nearly all the time. There may be up to three instances where you need to be louder or clearer. You have good eye contact with your group, only looking at me once or twice.	You are heard and understood by everyone outside the Fishbowl all the time. You look at the person you are responding to, as well as project your voice. You do not look at me, but instead use body language to convey interest.
Conversing **CCSS.ELA-Literacy. SL.8.1.d** Acknowledge new information expressed by others, and, when warranted, qualify or justify their own views in light of the evidence presented. /5	You don't talk to the group, but you might read something you have written down. You are not listening to the other members of the group. The comments are not connected to what is being said.	You are a good conversationalist. You are listening to and responding to those in the group. You state your opinions and are comfortable discussing this topic.	You are an excellent conversationalist, even going so far as to pull others who are quiet into the discussion. You are confident in your answers, but are great at synthesizing new information.

_____ **/15 Feedback:**

I ask the Resource Groups to identify what they think to be the most difficult questions and highlight keywords. The next step will be to separate them into ability groups.

Ability Groups

The detrimental impact of misused ability groups is widely reported, and I think it led to an overcorrection of never grouping students by ability, particularly after elementary school. Despite the obvious slots in middle and high schools based on ability—advanced and AP classes for example—teachers don't always feel comfortable grouping by ability within their classrooms. In many circles it isn't politically correct to even acknowledge the wide range of abilities, but instead a horrible "teach to the middle mentality" has taken the place of differentiation. The key to ability grouping is that it is not permanent, not announced, and each group is given a valuable and challenging task, suitable for the students at the particular table. The heterogeneous make-up used for the introductory and direct instruction phases of the unit does not make sense during this second phase of learning. If used correctly, ability groups allow students an opportunity to rehearse what they are learning. This is the best time to give formative assessments, create interventions, and provide support.

In order to "randomly" choose groups based on ability, I most often use tiered questions and Popsicle sticks. The Fishbowl questions, like most choices in my class, are organized by level of difficulty based on Bloom's taxonomy. Table 1 tasks should be knowledge based, with an emphasis on remembering and understanding. Table 2 tasks should be application of some sort. Table 3 should be analyzing. Table 4 should be an evaluative task. Table 5 should require students to create.

Label the sticks Table 1–5, based on the number of seats you have at each table. In one hand I put Table 1–3 sticks, representing the more concrete tasks. In the other hand, I put the Table 4 and 5 sticks that correlate to the higher order thinking tasks. As students come in, I offer the student the hand that is best for that student, *at that time.* It is important to note that each time groupings are done, the teacher should reassess which type of task is appropriate for that student *at that time* and remember to check her bias. We all try to be open-minded about students; it is easy to assume that a straight "A" student gets everything immediately, but in reality, when we notice a blip in his/her usual performance, we need to allow him/her an opportunity at the Table 1–3 tasks. The same is true for a struggling student; there should be times when we notice an uptick in performance, and we should "switch hands" to allow for that student to learn in a different environment.

You might be reading along right now, thinking, "Well, that's interesting, but surely this lady doesn't presume to know the precise level of *all* her students *all* the time." It's true, I have 127 students currently, so I'd be Wonder Woman if I knew precisely where my students are with a given topic all the time. I use formative data and my own observations and go with my gut; luckily, in two of my classes I have Special Education teachers who are even more observant than I am, frequently recognizing a strength or weakness that I had missed. Think of it this way: By grouping the tasks in Tables 1–3 and Tables 4–5, you generally won't be so far off that it is detrimental to the student. And, there's nothing wrong with eyeing the room when you start class and making a few switches. I always frame this in a positive way. For example, if Steven is going to sink at Table 5, I might say, "Steven, would you mind moving to Table 2 as a favor? You are great at social studies, so I think you'll add to that conversation." Of course you have to know your students well enough to give a compliment to make the move, but it's also perfectly OK to say, "Karen, you are in such a good mood today, spread the cheer with Table 1 please!" I've never had students figure out what I'm doing in the great balancing act, but I also recalibrate constantly, so even a mismatched grouping is only temporary.

Students work together within their groups to answer the question they've been tasked with. They use books and devices, they sometimes call their social studies teacher or the librarian, and they ask me lots of questions. They are encouraged to talk to students in other classes who are working on the same question. The goal in this acquisition stage is to make learning as authentic as possible for Digital Natives. Think about it: If you need to know something, you google it, post the question on Facebook, or run a hashtag search on Twitter. Why would we want to limit our students to finding the answers in a book? This means they will spend time googling things, taking notes on their tablets, pulling up pictures to go with the questions, or watching a video, but most importantly, they are not limited to the resources I have in my room. By allowing a no-holds-barred approach to gathering information, they are utilizing skills that will make them successful while also learning in a way that fits their normal, constantly connected lives, authenticating the task at hand as valuable.

When their table is called, students bring their notes with them to the discussion in the Fishbowl. The students on the outside are taking notes on a sheet I provide.

They know that their final objective test will contain these five questions. I include a spot to write down a "friendly face," who is a student whom the observers can follow up with later if there are gaps in the notes. Students are allowed to use these notes to help them during their final test. This practice encourages listening skills and rewards clarifying questions and good habits. This interdependence creates a collegiality that benefits all students. Each discussion has a moderator as well; this person reads the background prompt information, asks the questions, and is tasked with keeping the conversation moving and making sure that all members can be heard. The moderator also tries to help the group by prompting

Figure 2.3 *The Giver* Pre-reading Fishbowl Notes

Name: _____ Period: _____

_____/15 points classwork grade

Resource group topic	Important words and phrases, and definitions	Ideas that were interesting or surprising	If you were talking . . .
RG #1: What is a utopia? Friendly face: _____			
RG #2: Transforming the United States into a utopia Friendly face: _____			
RG #3: Bullying and power Friendly face: _____			
RG #4: Connotation and conclusions Friendly face: _____			
RG #5: Real utopias Friendly face: _____			

them to do things they know are being assessed. For example, if the conversation has taken a wild turn and is off on a tangent, the moderator might say, "Stephanie, can you bring us back to the text?" or "Jill, can you summarize what your group has said so far?" The reason I incorporate the moderator is that I am then freed up to provide quality feedback for each student and create an atmosphere where students talk to each other, not me.

How does our shy and quiet Kaylee fare in this situation? I'm not going to tell you she led every conversation or was 100% loud enough every time she spoke. However, we are talking about a student who had NEVER spoken in front of the class, not just in my class, but in *any* class. Yet the rehearsal time that she had in her ability group had allowed her time to try out her thoughts, listen to the points of others, and practice her conversational skills. The teachers in the room had spent time working with the groups to validate students as they tried out answers to complex questions in a low-risk environment. Better yet, as she participated in front of twenty-two other students, knowing that she was being assessed by both them and me, there was a new confidence to Kaylee that was immediately noticeable.

When I teased her about her transformation, I asked, "Aside from my amazing teacher magic, how did you go from this mega shy girl who would take zeros to *this*?"

> "When we first got our Resource Groups I was so glad it was people where I felt comfortable. I had my friend right next to me, just kinda helping me along," Kaylee explained.
> "Ok, that makes sense. But how did you feel when we moved into different groups to work on the questions to prepare for the Fishbowl?" I asked, referring to the ability grouping days. "The ones where you picked a Popsicle stick."
> "I was nervous, but I had already talked with my Resource Group, so I was ok. I had people who were cheering me along," Kaylee said.
> "What about the 'real Fishbowl' though—the one that was the test grade?" I asked, referring to the assessment stage, when students are randomly chosen to go in, making it an authentic conversation.
> "I guess, I don't know, I had practiced it before, so I could focus on talking instead of what to say. I already knew *what* to say," Kaylee reflected.

As Kaylee left, I felt that great rush of knowing you are doing the right thing, even if it is harder sometimes. It becomes clear that if we focus first on teaching *children*, rather than teaching *content*, really amazing growth can happen.

Is my classroom always a mecca of differentiation and smiling success? Absolutely not. Some days, it seems like all this grouping and regrouping is more organizationally challenging than it is worth. However, when I think about my own children, I am certain that I want their education to be responsive to their needs, and if it is a headache sometimes, so be it. Is my room always arranged in tables and working together like Santa's little elves, enjoying all this differentiation? No. Sometimes we are in vertical rows (assessment days), sometimes we are in horizontal rows (student presentations), and sometimes we are scattered around the room in a way that always looks so chaotic that I want to hang a sign saying, "Pardon the mess! Twenty-first-century learners doing their thing here!" When they are crouched in corners reading on their tablets and participating in a Google Docs journaling discussion, it isn't my need for order and organization that is being met, but their need for social interactions to enhance learning.

Social Reading Strategies

To me, reading has always been an intimate experience between my friends and me—you know, the characters in the book. You can't convince me that Meg Murry, Margaret Simon, and Laura Ingalls were not a part of my childhood circle of friends. Some of you may be best friends with Harry Potter or Hermione. Maybe Katniss Eberdeen is your soul sister. Now, though, I am seeing how a social experience could enhance reading, particularly for those who, unlike me (the self-proclaimed reading nerd), might not forge relationships with the characters. Instead, a community of readers can develop together in ways that are comfortable for Digital Natives. Equally exciting, this social experience can lead to collaborative writing.

I can tell you that "social reading" may seem like an oxymoron, but when students are engaged, there is nothing more logical, and that engagement leads to exceptional collaborative writing that students are proud of and invested in. After all, teachers have been trying for decades to move to more collaboration in their classrooms. However, once again—and almost always—students have found the solutions themselves, and 21st-century teachers should embrace the role of "obstacle mover" and "opportunity maker" and facilitate an approach to reading that is both social and personal, a juxtaposition worth exploring.

My goal is for students to guiltlessly experience the joy of reading unencumbered by the expectation of an analytical essay or the pressure to "close read"—both activities that I teach at other points in the year—as they are important skills and can be taught in inventive and interesting ways. However, I think that students must also be given a creative outlet for their responses to literature and that we'd all be better served if the link between reading and writing is severed on occasion. I've created "Bookclub," and it has worked well to enhance the experience for the book lovers who want to scream with every reading log AND the student who really doesn't want to read at all.

Figure 2.4 Bookclub

You are going to be having a great time this quarter as you read the same book as some of your friends in a "Bookclub." You'll be reading a book that your group chooses and having some amazing conversations while completing several activities to help you understand the book. You can work on these projects together or on your own, but I expect that the more people who are working on it, the more complex the final project will be. Trust me, you're going to love this. So, to begin, spend a few minutes reading through the FAQs (Frequently Asked Questions) and project choices before you bombard me with questions!

FAQs

What are the "projects"?

> Projects are activities that you complete with your Bookclub. The projects are meant to take many days, and span the entire novel. You should let your imagination be your guide. This is fun, but representative of who are you as a student.
> If you have a great idea for a project, shoot me an email, and propose what you'd like to do. The more descriptive you are, the more likely I'll say yes. I'll let you know within twenty-four hours.

What are the "graded discussions"?

> Each group will be given the "Not Your Mama's Lit Circle" role and discussion guide. There will be a Storyteller, Quizmaster, Number Cruncher, Image Examiner, and Jam Maker. I'll circulate and listen in on your discussions, and collect your notecards after the discussion. These are class participation grades. You will be having two of these graded discussions, and you'll need to pick a different role for the second one.

What are "reading and listening days"?

> This means that you will be silently reading or listening to your book. If you are choosing to listen, you need to follow along in your book. Download the book from the library, or I can help you get it. If you want, you can share one device. Bring earbuds. You don't need to take notes, unless it makes you happy.

What are "project workdays"?

> Project workdays are days that you are allowed to work on your projects. You may obtain a pass to anywhere in the building you need to go, as long as an adult agrees to it. I have had students who went to the library, did something musical, and even interviewed an administrator. You are always meant to represent our class. You have my trust—until you don't! Any negative report is an automatic suspension of travel.

Tell me again about "let imagination be your guide."

This is my favorite project. You are set free to a large extent to use your talents to talk about a book. Over the years, I've had amazing projects that I have designed and even more proposed projects that are mind-blowing. Here are some of the best-of-the-best:

—A map made entirely out of Lego bricks, probably 3,000 pieces, built to scale;
—A violin piece written and performed to represent the death of a character;
—A funeral for a character who dies but does not get a "proper burial";
—A performance of an original song written from the protagonist's perspective;
—A presentation of a web-based video game a student created using the plot of the novel;
—A rap written and performed for one character by another with full band;
—A film short;
—A fan fiction website;
—A scene of the book, acted out on the video, then played for the class.

What happens if we hate the book?

You can abandon the book in the first week; no worries. After that, your group will need to decide whether to find a new book; some who like it can stay. For example, two people stay with the book and three people find a new book.

What happens if I want to work alone?

That's totally cool with me. On group discussion days, I will check your role sheets—you'll need to do all the roles, and you'll get to go to the library since you've already "discussed" it on paper with yourself!

What happens if I want to quit my group?

You will need to let me know, and we can proceed from there. I'll keep your grades from the group, and going forward, the rest will be on your own.

What happens if I am absent?

That's the awesome part—you can work on this from anywhere, whenever you want. If you end up finishing your reading or projects, you may get a library pass or work on other homework.

What if we need extra time or a place to work?

You can get a pass to work in my room. Also, the librarian is also very flexible and knows about this project. Just get passes.

Project Choices:

Design a website

You or your group may use any platform you wish, but I use Wix. Your website should have five pages (at least) where you explore an aspect of the book. This is NOT a summary. You should start with a burning question or something you believe the author or character would want to share with the world. For example, the book *Hoot* might be an environmental activist site. You'd have a "Ways to Help" page, an "Endangered Species" page, a "Burrowing Owls" page, a "Petition to the City Planners" page, and a narrative page to explain your cause.

Recycled or upcycled project

Individually or as a group, recycle or upcycle items to create a piece of art or design something useful and innovative. The project needs to have a connection to your book. For example, if you read a book where the main character is a fashionista, you may do a clothing drive and then repurpose the clothes by sewing on collars, adding hems, turning jeans into a purse, and so forth. Then you should donate them to a person or to an organization. Remember, the more people involved, the bigger the donation should be.

Demonstration or "how-to" presentation or video

You or your group can do this "live" in person or make a video. Let's say you read *Gym Candy*. You can create a video about working out in healthy ways and how to build muscle. You would contrast your "how-to" with the use of steroids in the book, making clear how it impacted the character and would impact us.

Photojournalism

Photojournalists tell stories through pictures. Alone or together, you can bring in pictures, create a Prezi or PowerPoint, use Canva or Haiku Deck, but you'll need to make your story smack us in the face. Choose only photos that capture something essential or unique. This is not a summary or retelling of the story. Let's say you read *If I Stay*; you might create a slideshow of multiple perspectives of heaven, set to classical music that is mentioned in the book.

Interview an expert

Find someone who knows something you don't who is willing to talk to you, and pick his/her brain. Let's say you read *The Hunger Games*; find a video game designer who will talk to you about the viability of creating games like in the book. Find out why people are so obsessed with gaming. If doing this as a group, you'll each need to interview someone different, and compare what you learn.

Arrange and organize a guest speaker visit

This one is an individual project. Find someone who knows something you don't who is willing to talk to you and us. Let's say you read *The Hunger Games*; find a video game designer who will talk to us about the viability of creating games like in the book. Find out why people are so obsessed with gaming. Your guest may Skype, FaceTime, or do a Google Hangout with us, or come visit!

Collaborative writing

Design an opportunity for you and your group to write collaboratively. This means that you can do this on Google Docs or any other platform that works for you. For example, let's say you read *Sisterhood of the Traveling Pants*; your group might decide to write your own adventures such as *The Hoodie Diaries* or *The Secret Life of Ballet Shoes*.

New ending

Collaboratively write a new ending. This means that you can do this on Google Docs or any other platform that works for you. Your new ending should be substantially different, and between six and ten pages. If you want to write more, pick the six to ten pages you want me to assess.

Fan fiction

Collaboratively write fan fiction using elements of your novel, particularly the characters. Try to put the characters in interesting situations where you have to be inventive. For example, how would Tris from *Divergent* survive your Christmas dinner with your twenty-five relatives? This means that you can do this on Google Docs or any other platform that works for you. Your new ending should be substantially different, and between six and ten pages. If you want to write more, pick the six to ten pages you want me to assess.

Write a screenplay

Collaboratively or alone, adapt a scene or two of the story for film or stage. You'll need to research the appropriate way it is written, but there are lots of examples. One of my students who did this as a project option in 8th grade has gone on to film school!

After groups are formed—I allow them the freedom to choose, with five students being the maximum number—I make sure that students find the "just right" book for their group. The best way to do this is to work in conjunction with your library. Mrs. Rachel Brew, our library media specialist, has developed sets of "Bookclub" copies, in part as a result of this yearly project. This year, I found that students were very engaged with the video trailers she showed of the books.

The first important task, after students have chosen their books, is to chunk the book into sections and set due dates that students mutually agree upon. For example, do they want to read over weekends? What is a reasonable number of pages that they believe they could read during a Sustained Silent Reading period of ELA? I include this step under "Facilitate Good Choices" because students may find that the book is impossibly long, or that the book might not be meaty enough to use for this project. I encourage students, as I am monitoring this process, to consider sports schedules, concert dates, and family obligations as they do this very important first step.

Last year, I overheard one of my students say, "I don't want to read on Wednesdays. My dad picks me up that night, and I can't spend the time reading when I don't see him until the weekend." Another student, lamenting her complex track/National Junior Honor Society/chorus/confirmation class schedule, informed her group, "I think I have to read it in bigger chunks over the weekend. My week is stacked!"

To teachers, who are often the Type A orderly planners, this "chunking" of reading and calendar planning seems like a waste of time. Take it from one of those Type A planners who has a darling calendar with stickers representing everything from playdates to dentist appointments: Many students are not wired that way. In fact, I allow my generation of Digital Natives to use their calendar on their phones or electronic devices, and encourage them to sync with their parents. I also show them how to set reminders with alarms because while they may be tech savvy, they aren't all well versed in these more adult-focused apps.

I tend to be rather overt in my explanations for several reasons, the most vital two being the tremendous help it is for Special Education students and the importance of criteria for the projects. However, this Bookclub was initially designed for the month of state testing because schedule changes and my absences to score or proctor make-ups kept my students from enjoying continuity. I'll give the students the FAQs for Bookclub and have them read it; then we discuss the questions they have. They are genuinely excited to engage with a book and each other in this way.

During the unit, students read, participate in two graded discussions, create a project, and present it to the class. It is really important to be as specific as possible about the expectations and due dates because students (and teachers!) can become very overwhelmed when confronted with a huge amount of work. When they realize how the schedule will work, they are more likely to approach the book project with curiosity, not as something to hurry through and finish. The world has changed, and teaching must keep up with it. My own children, who are seven and ten, are my guides when it comes to creating units like Bookclub. Would they want to do it? Would they learn from it? What life skills are also practiced? Will they be engaged? I realized that there was a need for this type of social interaction when my son wanted to "write a book."

"So I'm timmy as you probably know it's my first full length book. This isn't a chapter book so don't start holing your breath. If you think I'm a good student RONG!" These are the words (mistakes and all) that

I just cut and pasted from Oliver's book that he is writing, called—you guessed it—*Timmy*. Now, if you are a parent of anyone under the age of twelve, you might realize that my son is not a child prodigy, but instead a very good mimic of the self-deprecating humor of Greg of *Diary of a Wimpy Kid* fame, mixed with a bit of James Patterson's Rafe from his *Middle School* series. My kids have listened to audiobooks their whole lives to fall asleep, so I've heard these two series myself about a million times.

What Oliver is actually doing can be classified as fan fiction, a genre that he discovered from the *Harry Potter* series, but has its roots in *Star Trek*. This genre has exploded, or as my ten-year-old daughter would say, "Yes mom, it's a *thing*." Readers—fans—have created all sorts of ways to respond to the literature they love, anything from podcasting to story extensions. As teachers, we need to embrace this desire for community in any way we can.

Collaboration Across Curriculums

I'm guessing that you don't have teachers from other subject areas dying to understand the best way to teach literacy skills in their classrooms. It isn't that they don't appreciate the importance of literacy, but they have their own content to teach, some of which is extremely dense. Just adding "another thing" to a teacher's plate is never going to lead to collaboration, but suggesting projects of mutual benefit might. Here are some ideas to share with your non-ELA friends that might lead to partnerships:

Science
What if students join forces on their lab report using Google Docs? Then, maybe they can share their findings with the class; and instead of having them speak from their seats, why not ask them to come to the front of the room? They will show ownership, enjoy the built in peer-to-peer competition, and have pride in their work. I can almost guarantee that it won't be long before one of those students wants to create a slide with a graph or chart to compare data. This generation of students has the ability to reach the entire world with their words via social media and the Internet, so we have to give them a larger viable audience within our classrooms instead of a one-person audience of just the teacher.

> **CCSS.ELA-Literacy.RST.6–8.7**
>
> Integrate quantitative or technical information expressed in words in a text with a version of that information expressed visually (e.g., in a flowchart, diagram, model, graph, or table).
>
> **CCSS.ELA-Literacy.RST.6–8.8**
>
> Distinguish among facts, reasoned judgment based on research findings, and speculation in a text.
>
> **CCSS.ELA-Literacy.RST.6–8.9**
>
> Compare and contrast the information gained from experiments, simulations, video, or multimedia sources with that gained from reading a text on the same topic.

Health

What if you changed the questions on the "Evidence Scavenger Hunt" to meet your content needs?

Figure 2.5 Activity 1: Evidence Scavenger Hunt

Read the claims below. Then, in the space below the claim, copy specific text from your book to support that claim. Include page numbers. Longer quotes can be shortened to a line or two, then add an ellipsis (. . .). Highlight or circle the word in the parenthesis that most creates an accurate sentence about your book or character.

The protagonist (IS) or (ISN'T) an average teenager.

_____

   pg. _____

There is more (PHYSICAL) OR (EMOTIONAL) turmoil in this book.

_____

   pg. _____

The protagonist's parents (DO) or (DON'T) understand him/her.

_____

   pg. _____

The protagonist is (SOCIAL) or (RECLUSIVE) or (SHY) or (ECCENTRIC) or (_____). You can pick more than one.

_____

    pg. _____

The central conflict is (person vs. person), (person vs. self), (person vs. nature), (person vs. society), or (person vs. machine).

_____

    pg. _____

This activity would be great to explore the ways media messages lure children in unhealthy directions. Challenge students to find evidence of body shaming, gender stereotyping, and socioeconomic bias in advertising, and they'll be thinking deeply, exploring important health concepts, and having conversations that can impact them for the rest of their lives—the reason we got into this teaching thing in the first place!

> **Health Education Standard 2**
> Students will demonstrate the ability to access valid health information and health-promoting products and services.
>
> **Health Education Standard 4**
> Students will analyze the influence of culture, media, technology, and other factors on health.

Social Studies

What if the "timeline activity" (Figure 2.6) were reworded to explain the suffrage movement?

    Assign students different regions in the country, let them create timelines, and discuss the implications that are revealed. Not only would key distinctions become clear to students, but you'd be meeting standards as well. Again, literacy is a schoolwide effort in the current educational climate.

Strategic Groupings ◆ 51

Figure 2.6 Activity 2: Timeline Activity

Create a timeline for your book so far. You will need to think of ten events that have happened that you believe may be important to the meaning, may foreshadow an event to come, or may be important to demonstrate characterization. Use page numbers.

You may choose how to represent the events. It can be on a timeline, in sequence. It could be through a series of pictures that you connect, or it could be designed to show the size of the events compared to one another.

CCSS.ELA-Literacy.RH.6–8.7

Integrate visual information (e.g., in charts, graphs, photographs, videos, or maps) with other information in print and digital texts.

Math

What if the "Plus and Minus Tool for Graded Discussions" (Figure 2.7) were a part of the classroom routine?

Figure 2.7 Plus and Minus Tool for Graded Discussions

You are each earning a classwork grade for your discussion today. I'll be observing and listening in. Ignore me when I'm nearby, unless you have a question, but even then I'll probably redirect it to you. This is a student-led day where I facilitate your awesomeness!

I will be giving you a (+) for the positive behaviors observed in the discussion or a (–) for any of the behaviors observed that are not appropriate. In the end, you'll have a chance to reflect and help me to see what grade you think you earned.

Positive Behaviors

    Asking a question
    Responding thoughtfully to a classmate's question or comment
    Having top-notch notecards
    Listening respectfully
    Using the text to support your opinions
    Reminding classmates to stay on topic/pay attention
    Helping a shy or quiet student get involved
    Using each other's names in the conversation ("I think that sounds good, Joe")
    Rephrasing what the person before you said ("Joe suggested that the character is evil")
    Politely disagreeing ("I don't see it the way Joe does; I actually think the character is sad")
    Taking academic or social risks (sharing something that may be a little different)

Negative Behaviors

    Being unprepared to ask questions
    Interrupting others when they are talking
    Not participating
    Doing anything that is not related to this discussion (off-topic chats, other homework)
    Talking over a classmate
    Being rude, insensitive, or making fun of another's comments/opinions
    Disrupting class or distracting classmates
    Reading from your notes without eye contact

Highlight any of the (+) behaviors that I may have missed. Share any comments on the back.

When students are working collaboratively to solve a problem, we raise the stakes when they are also aware that we notice how they conduct themselves in a discussion. This particular tool has improved on-task behaviors in my class and created a more academic environment. I've graded class discussions for several years now, and though I'm not a carrot-and-stick kind of teacher, sometimes students value the things we choose to grade. With the additional emphasis on creating arguments, this technique makes sense. The traditional literary circle has to be revisited with expanded roles and 21st-century skills embedded.

Figure 2.8 Not Your Mama's Lit Circle

Twice during our Bookclub unit, I will be grading a discussion that you are having. I'll be using the attached rubric. During our first organizational meeting you will need to randomly choose who is doing what task for the first discussion. You may make it random any way you choose—youngest to oldest, alphabetical by middle name, blinking contests, and so forth. The second discussion works the same way, but you have to have a different role. PREPARE OUTSIDE OF CLASS!

Prepare for your discussions on notecards. I'll collect them after your discussion. Write your name and the role you had on the top line of each card.

And yes, I am aware that these are "weird" things to do and are certainly not like "normal" lit circles. You'll see. The conversation will surprise you.

Storyteller

> Your job is going to be to "tell the story" of what has happened in the book so far. This means you'll need to have a beginning, middle, and end. You'll need to include the main characters, as well as include important events. It may sound silly.

For example:

> Once upon a time there was this girl, Tris, who never felt like she fit in with her family. As she grew older it became clear why: She was *Divergent*.

If you'd like, you can do this on your device as a voice memo or other recording.

After you share your story, ask the group what they thought of your retelling. What did you leave out? What did you include that someone forgot? Are there any moments that seem like foreshadowing?

Quizmaster

> Your job is going to be to make up a list of ten questions that you'll "quiz" your group on. Try to have a balance between "right there" questions and ones that might take some deeper thought.

For example:

> Where does the protagonist live? ("right there" question)
> What circumstances led to her family having to move? (deeper thinking)

Number Cruncher

> Your job is to "crunch" all the numbers you see or learn about in the book. I know, it seems weird, but it will help you to approach the book in a different way. You'll need ten to share with your group and see what they think.

For example:

> Zach has gone to twelve schools before 8th grade. (informs us about his past)
> Alicia makes $7.00 an hour to babysit, and she works three hours a day, five days a week, so she'll earn $105 a month. She gives it to her mom to help pay the bills. (informs us about her home life and socioeconomic status)

Image Examiner

> Your job is going to share with the group at least three images that you have noticed. Authors embed information when they use an image over and over. The trick is to pay attention and then figure out what the author is trying to tell the reader. Make sure to ask your group what they think.

For example:

> Every time Tracy talks, she says it out loud, but she also mumbles to herself and shakes her head. (maybe she doesn't feel heard?)
> Jason is always taking pictures on his old and battered camera, which is huge. He won't use his cell phone to take pictures. I imagine him hiding behind the camera. (maybe he is holding on to the past or is actually trying to hide so he doesn't have to talk to anyone)

Jam Maker

> Your job is to make a jam, as in a list of songs, not jelly. The songs should go with the book so far. To make your mix, you'll need to come up with five songs that "fit" the book. Jot down the title and at least a little of the song, or the chorus. If it is school appropriate, you can also play it for your group. Bring earbuds or borrow headphones.

For example:

> Bea Miller's "Force of Nature" is the best song for the protagonist because she is experiencing being swept away by Todd, but knows it won't last.
> "And I know I'll be broken when it is over. . . ."

> **CCSS.Math.Practice.MP3 Construct viable arguments and critique the reasoning of others.**
>
> Mathematically proficient students understand and use stated assumptions, definitions, and previously established results in constructing arguments. They make conjectures and build a logical progression of statements to explore the truth of their conjectures.

Learning From Our Mistakes

It isn't easy to try something new, for sure. The learning curve is always scary. Who wants to be figuring it out as we go along? But we can push past our hesitancies and embrace the growth mindset we want for our students. Modeling "fails" (which do happen) are important for our students to see. What did we do when we screwed up the numbers or forgot there was an assembly on the same day we planned a Fishbowl? We show students that solving the problems that arise is as important as being able to follow the smooth sailing schedule that is in our plan books.

Being transparent about overcoming bumps in the road will help you move children toward self-discovery. Don't avoid new flexible classroom arrangements just because they're challenging; have conversations about what you're thinking and learning, and help students learn to reflect on their own thoughts and learning too, so they can discover their unique skills.

We all feel the test pressure. Yet we have to remember they aren't sheep, and we're not shepherds. Do you want to know why that mindset has to go? Because sheep don't know how to get out of a rut they create from walking the same path. They actually walk it so long that they break their ankles or physically cannot climb out, never escaping their circumstances. They are paralyzed without being told what to do, and that flies in the face of the needs our students have in a global society. No matter how we feel about the Common Core or Project Based Learning, or ability grouping, I think we can all agree on one thing: no ruts for our students.

Your Turn

How are you going to organize students for learning?

- *Every classroom is different.* What special considerations should you remember as you strategically group your students?

- *Carol Tomlinson says students can be different in their readiness, interest, and learning profile.* How can you observe these differences and group accordingly?
- *Social reading can improve performance.* Which reading assignments can you alter to allow social interaction?
- *Collaboration works for any curriculum.* Is there another teacher you can work with to collaborate?
- *Strategic groupings are never permanent.* How often do you think you want to rearrange your groups?

3

Word Study

Personalizing Vocabulary

I love words. Fizzle. Juxtaposition. Hummus. Toasty. Brazen. I love learning a new word that fits a situation so perfectly that no further explanation is necessary—in the Northeast, we had Snowvember last year. I love to hate some words—selfie, Tweeps (your "peeps" on Twitter), and planking. How then, was it possible, for me to hate teaching vocabulary? Probably because I wasn't looking at vocabulary as the study of words, but instead the list of words that we had to study.

Over the years I've tried everything from looking up the definition, using the word in a sentence, or copying it three times—to more inventive activities like drawing a picture, writing a synonym, writing an example, and writing a non-example. None of these strategies amounts to educational malpractice, and in fact, taken together, could constitute a pretty decent approach—if you planned to teach one word. However, teachers know that there is a never-ending list of words our students might need to know, and before we can even think about effective methods to differentiate, we need to figure out how to narrow down that list. This chapter contains time-saving resources and step-by-step explanations for teaching *words*, not just vocabulary lists.

Sneak Peek

In this chapter, we'll look at . . .

- *the difference between receptive and expressive vocabulary*
- *methods to choose the best words for your specific purpose*
- *how to stop assaulting your students with vocabulary lists*
- *ways to use visual aids*
- *steps to integrate vocabulary instruction*
- *how to use tiered lists to narrow down vocabulary*
- *ideas to create a personalized word study*
- *methods to track progress and assess vocabulary acquisition*
- *strategies to handle domain-specific vocabulary.*

Receptive and Expressive Vocabulary

Before assigning vocabulary to students—no matter which strategy or strategies you employ—decide if you want the word to become a part of their *receptive* vocabulary or their *expressive* vocabulary. I'll address expressive vocabulary further on, but first: Receptive vocabulary refers to the words that a student knows when heard or read, but the student can't really explain to others or work with the word out of context or use it originally. More likely, it is a part of a schema surrounding a topic. For example, "polypeptide" is a word that I know I've learned, I know it is related to biochemistry, and because I know "poly" means many, I have it in my head that it is a structure of many parts that has to do with the "stuff" I learned in chemistry. That's not the most eloquent understanding of the word, and I definitely can't teach it or use it, but if I were to read it or hear someone say it, I'd have enough of an understanding to follow the rest of the conversation or use context to decipher the sentence.

How Much Time Do I Spend on a Vocabulary Word?

Depending upon the subject, the purpose for learning the words can change. In ELA, when I teach "The Landlady," a creepy story that includes a morbid old woman who enjoys taxidermy, we encounter the word "formaldehyde." It is enough for me to say, "Formaldehyde is a chemical used in the process of taxidermy"—which is all the students would need to know for *my* purposes. If I were the chemistry teacher, I might need students to have a much more complex understanding of the chemical, which would require a more intensive study of the word, leading to the understanding that formaldehyde is an organic compound, and the chemical formula of formaldehyde is CH_2O. Yet, as the ELA teacher, if I have students invest more than a small amount of time familiarizing themselves with this type of word, I'm spending an inordinate amount of energy on a low-frequency, low-mileage word—meaning that in ELA, they aren't going to come across the word often and won't find a use for it very often either.

Vocabulary Versus Word Study

I'll be the first to admit that I used to scour text, congratulating myself that I could pick out all the words my students wouldn't know. Though that is helpful information, and instruction should be modified accordingly, I was wasting my time creating activities and assessments, practically assaulting them with words! This is counterproductive for two reasons: One, it doesn't work for most students, and two, they will hate learning words. After lackluster results, I knew I had to make vocabulary "fit" everything else I do in my classroom: showing respect for individual student needs. Somehow, in all the conversation about tiers, academic vocabulary, SAT lists, and assessment language, I had gotten away from what I knew mattered: Words are powerful and amazing, and can be the vehicle by which students can change their worlds. Now, instead of even talking about "vocab," I approach this huge task from a "word study" perspective, and though it might only appear to be a semantics change, it is effective. However, we can't simply leave those receptive vocabulary words out of our instruction, or that could prohibit student learning. One suggestion is to give students a mini-dictionary (or create one, depending on your time and needs) to use as they read. Some teachers create a Word Study notebook, and this dictionary can be glued in there for reference. Include on that list the words that you will be overtly teaching as well, but put those in all capital letters. This way, students will be made aware of the words that you think are important, and the words that they will need to learn in their word study.

After determining which words are OK to leave as *receptive*, the next step is to focus on the words that you wish them to add to their *expressive* vocabulary—these are the words that you want them to use with automaticity, words they can use with ease, understand thoroughly, and need to know to help them be better communicators.

Figure 3.1 "The Landlady" Word Study Dictionary

As we read "The Landlady," we will encounter words that are unusual or unfamiliar. Many of these words are included here. Some of these words will be helpful to understand the story, and some of the words are valuable because they will help us throughout the year. Those that will be continually assessed this year are **BOLDED** and **CAPITALIZED**. We'll work on those as a part of our word study.

> Accurately: correctly
> Cathedral: the main building of a part of a Catholic diocese
> **COMPEL**: to force someone to do something
> Congenial: someone who is likable because they are like you
> Conjure: to make something appear or seem to appear, as if by magic
> **EMANATE**: to come out from a source, like breath or an odor
> Façade: the front of a building
> Glance: to look at quickly and casually
> **ILLUMINATE**: to light up or shine a light upon, making things clearer
> Inclining: leaning forward
> Lapse: an occurrence where a person behaves badly, usually for a short time
> Linger: to stick around for longer than the expected time
> **PEER**: to look closely and carefully at something (second definition—person of the same group)
> **PROCEEDING**: a legal action when you go in front of a court
> Rapacious: always wanting more money or possessions
> Splendid: out of the ordinary, very fancy or fabulous
> Tantalize: to continually taunt with something very desirable, but never give it to the person.

Please complete a Word Study for each of the **BOLD** and **CAPITALIZED** words. You may use any strategy we have learned. These words will be assessed.

Explicit Instruction

The expressive vocabulary needs to be explicitly taught, but the way students study the word can vary. To explicitly teach the word, I use a PowerPoint, Prezi, or Haiku Deck, but any slide show will work fine. The first slide you create is of a striking picture that will make an impact on students. For example, for "The Landlady" I'd use the following:

> Compel: a picture of a bride and groom shoving cake in each other's face
> Emanate: a picture of someone with bad breath
> Illuminate: a picture of the Disney character Lumiere
> Peer: a big eye with a magnifying glass
> Proceeding: a courthouse scene.

The more silly, dramatic, or novel the picture is, the better. If the students are laughing, you are doing this part correctly. At this time, encourage students to share stories. The more social this segment is, the more successfully you are embedding a memory to go along with the word itself, essentially creating a second bookmark in the child's brain to complement the direct instruction. This will allow students multiple methods of retrieval when searching for the word in their long- and short-term memories. I know that it can seem counterintuitive to let students talk so much during direct instruction, but the more invested and engaged they are, the more likely they will be to remember the word. This approach is supported by the goals of CCSS because according to the narrative accompanying the standards, "The standards call for students to grow their vocabularies through a mix of conversation, direct instruction, and reading."

Next, create a duplicate slide, but this time include a text box at the top with the word and the definition. After introducing the word, ask each group to create a sentence using the word. I like to do this on whiteboards. Allow a student from each table to stand and share the sentence, making sure to rotate through all students. I typically have five words that I want to add to their expressive vocabulary at a time, so this works well at the tables of five. Finally, students are asked to complete a "word study" of each word. There are multiple methods to choose from, and they may use a single strategy or a combination of strategies. I make sure students know that they will be sharing, and that I will choose some of their word studies to create a review sheet for class. It is another layer of creating a class culture of learning and risk taking for all students.

Use It or Lose It

These words are continually assessed, not solely on a vocabulary "quiz," but as we weave them into our conversations. I post the words on a "Words We Know" wall and make a huge deal when they use the words in class. I ask them to circle the words in their writing, and often prompt them with questions like, "Which three words that we know would fit well in our essay?" This helps students cluster the words into categories and make connections between and among words. We study the words all year, and I use these words in my communication with them, sometimes working them in to directions, other times as a part of a test question, and often dropping them into conversation. It is estimated that a person must hear, see, and/or use a word between ten and thirty times before it becomes a part of their expressive vocabulary—and that is with conscious effort. The more layering we can do, the better.

Tiered Lists and Common Core Shifts

Another approach is using the Three-Tier Framework, developed by Isabel Beck, Margaret McKeown, and Linda Kucan, where you decide how to narrow down which vocabulary words to teach by determining if the word is Tier 1 (words that students would acquire naturally, known words like "cat" or "table"), Tier 2 (words that are high utility and cross subject areas, such as unfamiliar words like "prediction" or "maintain"), or Tier 3 (words that are domain specific, such as the aforementioned "polypeptide"). The highest utility, highest mileage words are the best words to explicitly teach. That is not to say that we can't elect to teach Tier 3 words; of course we need to teach words that will add to the sum of student knowledge within our specific domains. However, we need to be choosy about the words we wish to study with our students, and there is nothing wrong with letting students know the difference between a word that is mostly a "science word," or "social studies word" and a word that they're likely to hear in many classes.

The Common Core State Standards website, http://www.corestandards.org, explains the key shifts this way: "Closely related to text complexity and inextricably connected to reading comprehension is a focus on academic vocabulary: words that appear in a variety of content areas (such as *ignite* and *commit*)." We need to create opportunities for students to expand their vocabularies, and until subject areas approach vocab lists as word study, we will continue to have students memorize for the short term, but never add the words to their expressive vocabulary.

> **CCSS.ELA-Literacy.L.8.6**
>
> Acquire and use accurately grade-appropriate general academic and domain-specific words and phrases; gather vocabulary knowledge when considering a word or phrase important to comprehension or expression.

Personalized Word Study

The most differentiated method of word study is a personalized list. I like this method very much, but I can understand why teachers are wary. If we, as professionals, are having a hard time figuring out how to teach vocabulary, how can a child do it? Are students operating on such a highly attuned metacognitive level that they are aware of the words they don't know? Some may be, that is certain; but in most cases, it takes specific instruction around the topic of word study for students to understand how they should choose their own words. If you feel your classroom is ready for deep discussion around words, this may be an option for you. Really, the decision is how much time you want to spend on word study in your classroom.

For much of the year, I dedicate Mondays to word study. Forty minutes of my 200 minutes each week are devoted to talk about words—this is dedicated time when I teach Greek and Latin roots, words that we'll need to know for what we are reading, and domain-specific words. In most cases, Mondays are really a form of pre-teaching. If I am going to be talking about suspense on Wednesday, then on Monday I'm going to make sure that my students understand the associated vocabulary: rising action, complication, dissonant (I like to talk about the dissonant notes in the *Jaws* movie score to explain suspense), jeopardy (writers build suspense by putting characters in jeopardy), tension, and metaphor.

> **CCSS.ELA-Literacy.L.8.4.b**
> Use common, grade-appropriate Greek or Latin affixes and roots as clues to the meaning of a word (e.g., *precede, recede, secede*).
>
> **CCSS.ELA-Literacy.L.8.5**
> Demonstrate understanding of figurative language, word relationships, and nuances in word meanings.
>
> **CCSS.ELA-Literacy.L.8.5.a**
> Interpret figures of speech (e.g., verbal irony, puns) in context.

I feel comfortable switching to a personal vocabulary list around half-year. Will my students still learn the domain-specific words like "rising action"? Yes, but *they* will be the ones who discover which words they want to study. Instead of having word study on Mondays, I move it to Fridays. Students come to class with their devices, I provide dictionaries and laptops, and we do our word study at the same time—but individually. They use the Word Study Sheet to formalize their work.

Figure 3.2 Word Study Vocabulary Choices

Complete one of these word study activities in your notebook for each word. Remember, once you do this, the word is fair game for any future assessment. You will see these words again, and again, and again, I promise! *Any option may be done by hand or digitally. I'll use your ideas to create a class study sheet.*

- *Graffiti*: Draw the word in bubble letters or stencil it. Put the definition in your own words underneath it. Draw at least three other things that remind you of the word or definition. For example, "compel" might be your mom making you go to bed and hand over your phone. Color all white space to make the picture pop.
- *Cartoon*: Create a cartoon that will connect the word to the meaning. For example, for the word "emanate," you might draw a smell coming from a man's big, stinky feet. The more ridiculous, the better. Make sure you write a sentence using the word correctly.
- *Word Anatomy*: Create an anatomy of the word by breaking it into parts, indicating prefixes, affixes, and suffixes. For example, for "proceeding," break it down like this:

    PRO (for something) + CEED (to pass or go beyond) + ing (suffix "happening")

Then explain how the anatomy matches up with the actual dictionary definition. In this case, imagine a court case going before a judge. Use an online dictionary to help you.

Word Association: Create a word web of pictures, phrases, or descriptions of mental pictures. For example, I'd place the word "illuminate" in the center of a lightbulb. In one bubble, I'd draw the picture of Lumiere, in another picture I'd draw a sunshine with rays flying off it, and in the last bubble I'd write the quote, "Let love illuminate the way."

Double Trouble: This option is only for words that have two meanings. You are going to create a mental picture (story in your head). For example, for the word "peer," you can imagine a peer (your friend) peering (looking) at your new outfit with a really big eye, eying you up and down. You don't have to draw it, but you can. Just make sure that your words will get the idea across to someone else.

Students will come prepared with their lists, and I will give them time to share with each other. If someone is able to help someone else with a word, that's all the better. After they've settled in and chatted about what words they chose, I set them to work in "quiet mode." They know this means that they are free to chat very quietly about what we are working on, or they are free to put on their earbuds and work on this alone. As much as I like the idea of students sitting around debating the best way to describe what "flummoxed" means, the reality is that there are some students who will always want to just get vocabulary done. I try to spark conversations with those students about the words they've chosen. However, I love collaboration enough to never force it upon a child.

Assessing Personalized Lists

One caveat to individual vocabulary instruction is that traditional assessments are impossible to manage if a room full of students is interacting with personalized lists. For me, that means that for my students to add only five words a week, multiplied by the five classes I teach, with an average of twenty-five students, there would be 625 new words! If you want to explore this non-traditional approach, you're going to need to discard the idea of a vocabulary quiz that can be corrected while you watch television—multiple choice, fill in the blank, word banks, and matching are out the window. Don't get me wrong, I'm always willing to use these methods formatively when dealing with domain-specific words, but if we are giving students the responsibility of choosing their own words, there is no reason they can't choose how we assess their understanding.

Show What You Know

An individualized vocabulary list requires a more flexible approach to assessment and provides the perfect opportunity for differentiation. The Show What You Know: Individualized Vocabulary Assessment is a way to track the progress of your students formatively and summatively, all in one place.

Figure 3.3 Show What You Know: Individualized Vocabulary Assessment

You will need to collect twenty words this quarter that you wish to master. How you choose to master these words will be largely up to you, as you will have several choices. You'll need to choose *one activity from Column A for EACH word and one activity from Column B to show that you know the twenty words*. You may do all of the same from Column A, or mix it up as you like. If your activity requires my time, make a brief (five minutes will do) appointment with me. If you are giving me something to look at, put it in a zip lock baggie with the name and your period number. You may hand it in any time between now and the last Friday before the end of the quarter.

Column A (Formative)	Column B (Summative)
Create a vocabulary notecard with the word's denotation, connotation, and a sentence.	Create a quiz for all of your words. It must use three types of questions such as multiple choice, matching, etc. Hand in a blank quiz and the answer key.
Create a 3D representation of the word. Make sure the definition is somewhere on the object.	Write a story, article, essay, newspaper article, lab report, or other written piece using all the words you have chosen. It has to be coherent; don't force the words to fit. Highlight the words.
Create a voice memo on your device saying the word, the denotation, the connotation, and using it in a sentence.	Create a "fill in the blank" story or passage using all of your words. What you write must make sense, and the sentences should contain clear context clues to help the reader fill in the blanks with the correct word. The word bank should be on the top. Hand in a blank one and a completed one.
Use the word in a sentence. Teach yourself to say the sentence in two other languages. Google Translate or our language teachers can help.	Create a rap or song with all of the words in it. Perform it for our class, videotape it, or send me a voice file. Make sure that the words are used in a way that their meaning is clear—not a list, for example.

Column A (Formative)	Column B (Summative)
Study the word's etymology (the history of the word and how it has changed over time). Share what you learn on a notecard.	Create a graphic that categorizes your words in some way. It could be origin, meaning, where you found the words, number of syllables, or something else you notice. You will need to have at least two categories. Write a paragraph for each category, explaining your choice.
Videotape yourself teaching the word to another person. Make sure that the other person participates.	Random quiz with me. Make an appointment. Bring with you a notecard with each word written on it, folded twice over to make a square. You'll place all the words in the hat, pull five out and explain them to me.
Create a jingle about the word. Sing it to me or send me a video or audio message.	Create a game that uses all your words. The game must rely on players' knowledge of the words—denotations, connotations, sentences, word origin, etc.

List all of your words here:

_____ _____ _____ _____ _____
_____ _____ _____ _____ _____
_____ _____ _____ _____ _____
_____ _____ _____ _____ _____

The main attraction of this activity sheet is the novelty of the activities. Students aren't usually asked to take charge of learning vocabulary, so when tasked with it and given some choice in the matter, they are enthusiastic. As always, the logistics for this type of activity are tricky, but well worth it.

How you use this sheet depends on how deeply you want to participate in their vocabulary acquisition process (Column A) and their culminating task (Column B). I print out a blank roster for each class. As I see or receive Column A activities, I give them an actual tally mark. If an activity for a word is wrong, I record an X, but make sure the student understands before moving on. At the end, I add up all tally marks and multiply by five points. I usually count it as a quiz grade, but it can easily be multiple classwork or homework grades. I just keep the list on a clipboard and students share what they are doing. It puts the responsibility on them, but it also creates a certain chaotic burden on the teacher as well. I'm often on the way to lunch when someone wants to give me Column A tasks or tell me about it. It makes for a word-rich environment, that's for sure, but it can also be overwhelming. In the end, though, students are learning more authentically, and I'm not grading vocab quizzes every week.

> **CCSS.ELA-Literacy.L.8.4.c**
> Consult general and specialized reference materials (e.g., dictionaries, glossaries, thesauruses), both print and digital, to find the pronunciation of a word or determine or clarify its precise meaning or its part of speech.
>
> **CCSS.ELA-Literacy.L.8.4.d**
> Verify the preliminary determination of the meaning of a word or phrase (e.g., by checking the inferred meaning in context or in a dictionary).

This activity also keeps students focused on the chunk of twenty words, giving them plenty of opportunities to really "get to know" the words and how they are used in different contexts. I want them to spend some time with the words, and have those exposures necessary to move the word into their expressive vocabulary.

The Column B tasks are all ways to summatively assess the student's knowledge of his/her list. All of the activities listed require higher order thinking skills without rote memorization, and require students to stretch their understanding of the words by using them all in a single task. Maybe I've sold you on this idea of an amazing word study journey, personalized for all; cue the inspirational music. And then, you probably start thinking, "Wait, but what about . . . ?" and a face comes to mind, and then another. There are some students who don't seem exactly cut out for making decisions about their curriculum.

Training Students to Choose Their Own Vocabulary

Of course you are right, which is why we have to train students to assess what they know and inspire them to find words that they need. Walk students through the "Choose Your Own . . . Vocabulary?!" tool to help students approach vocabulary acquisition in a metacognitive way.

Word Study ◆ 69

Figure 3.4 Choose Your Own . . . Vocabulary?!

How do you know which words to choose for your personalized word list? You'll need to do some thinking and answer a few questions as you pick your words to study.

Have I ever heard this word before?

If yes . . .	*If no . . .*
Do I understand what the word means exactly?	Look up the word. Would I use this word?
Can I use it in a sentence?	When would this word help me out?
Would I be willing to use it in conversation?	What other similar words do I know?
Can I explain the connotation?	Does this word interest me?
If you answered **yes** to all four questions, **find a new word**.	If you are **interested**, go for it! You've **found a word!**

If you answered **no** to all of the questions, you have **found a word**!
If you answered **no** to at least some of the questions, you **MIGHT have found a word**.
If you aren't intrigued, start over!

This methodology is a good guide, but sometimes there are words that you simply need to know. Maybe you are learning to knit and need to add *purl* (not the jewel "pearl") to your vocabulary. Or maybe you are trying a new sport, and you really need to understand what the coach means when he says, "If you see someone set a *pick* for you, you better take the chance." Learning those words will be easier because you care about them and you can cluster them under a certain idea—knitting or lacrosse.

Remember, don't sell yourself short! Pick words that you don't know or you'll hate this assignment and won't learn new words. Now that would be *atrocious* and a *travesty*, right? If you don't know what those words mean, that might be a good place to start!

Students then use the "Personal Vocabulary" activity for each word.

Figure 3.5 Personal Vocabulary

Name:	**Word:**
I found this word → *Inquisitive* I heard Mr. Jones say this about me.	I found this word →
The specific **context** → *She really is an inquisitive girl.*	The specific context →

(continued on the next page)

Figure 3.5 Continued

Name:	Word:
I think it means → *I ask a bunch of questions.*	I think it means →
The **denotation** is → *Adj. Inclined to investigate; eager for knowledge*	The denotation is →
The **connotation** is → *Positive. Interested and wants to learn.*	The connotation is →
Sentence that shows meaning → *The small boy at the museum was very inquisitive about the dinosaurs.*	Sentence that shows meaning →
Mental picture → *I imagine me taking a quiz and knowing the answers because I am so inquisitive.*	Mental picture →

Context: the situation the word is used in, specifically the other words or sentences around it.
Denotation: dictionary definition of the word (include the part of speech).
Connotation: the feelings associated with the word (include positive, negative, or both depending on the context).
Mental picture: create a story in your head, visualize it, then describe it.

I don't photocopy twenty of these sheets; instead, this sheet becomes a template for students to use in their notebooks. If you still feel uncomfortable, it is also fine to limit the choices for some students. For example, if a student isn't capable of making these decisions, ask her to bring in all the words she needs for any of her classes and help her choose from those. Sometimes too much choice is paralyzing, particularly for struggling students.

What Do I Do With Those Domain-Specific Words?

Domain-specific vocabulary in some areas makes all the difference in a student's success. If a Social Studies student is not familiar with the word "treason," for example, it can impact his understanding of an entire unit. The worst thing we can do for students who need to learn a big set of vocabulary words is to barrage them with the words all at once. I still remember being told to read a chapter in Social Studies, write down all the bold words, look them up in the glossary, and copy the definitions. Sometimes this meant as many as twenty words. Looking back, I was a compliant student, so I did the work, but I never looked at this as learning *words*. No one ever pointed out that "monopoly" contained the root "mono," meaning alone or one, and explained how this matches the definition. This isn't to say that Social Studies teachers—or any other teacher for that matter—must be a Greek and Latin scholar, but when possible we should give students keys to learning words.

> **CCSS.ELA-Literacy.RH.6–8.4**
> Determine the meaning of words and phrases as they are used in a text, including vocabulary specific to domains related to history/social studies.

If your domain does require an extensive number of vocabulary words, the first thing to do is to cluster the words, not by the order they are mentioned in the chapter, but organically. A great introductory activity is a wordsplash. Divide students into groups of four or five. Give each table a sheet that contains the vocabulary words that they will see in the unit. Make it a "splash" by scattering the words around, or you can create a word cloud electronically on sites such as Wordle or Tagxedo. For example, if you were previewing a chapter on photosynthesis, you might include the following words: light, chlorophyll, water, oxidation, sunlight, absorption, carbon dioxide, stomata, oxygen, vapor, and transpiration. Have students group the words in any way they think makes sense, taking time to "guesstimate" the definitions in writing because several of those words are a part of their receptive vocabulary.

Next, have students leave their paper on their table and have them rotate to the next table. When they sit down, using a different colored pencil or pen, they should add to what is written, or suggest other possibilities for clustering. For example, some students may chunk chlorophyll, carbon dioxide, and oxygen because they think they are all gases. When the next group of students rotates to that table, one of those students can write "chlorophyll is a pigment, which makes it a solid." Eventually, when students have rotated through all of the other tables, the class can come to a consensus. This is when you reveal the definitions to students. The advantage of this exploratory approach to vocab acquisition is that it is inquiry based and collaborative. Some people worry that students will need to "unlearn" something that was discussed in the groups incorrectly. Clearly this could present a problem, but in my experience, students are pretty adept at using their collective knowledge to generate correct (or nearly correct) definitions. Better yet, the conversations have contextualized the words for students, giving them the best opportunity to move them into their expressive vocabulary.

> **CCSS.ELA-Literacy.RST.6–8.4**
> Determine the meaning of symbols, key terms, and other domain-specific words and phrases as they are used in a specific scientific or technical context relevant to *grades 6–8 texts and topics*.

Students Teaching Students

Another approach is to have students teach each other the words. Divide the words up equally. Challenge each group to come up with a skit, catchphrase, or picture that will help everyone remember the definition. Provide students with dictionaries or allow them to use their devices to come up with the correct definition, but insist that they put them in their own words. I promise that once math students have demonstrated "additive identity" or "inverse operations," they will remember what happened in class, which will then link to the actual definition that they need to know. We must always capitalize on the relationships that students have with each other to encourage risk taking and having fun in the classroom. Until students are comfortable, they won't be able to acquire new vocabulary from their peers—which is a prime way for them to add to their vocabularies.

In one of my first years of teaching AP Literature, I assigned each student a vocabulary word. That student had to provide a way for the class to remember the definition. One of my students had a brilliant idea to teach his assigned phrase, "internal monologue." Steve stood in the front of the room, pushed play on the tape deck (this was a long time ago!), and as a voice began speaking on the tape, he started talking very seriously to the class, explaining the definition of interior monologue. As we listened, we gradually realized that the voice on the tape was also Steve, expressing his stream-of-consciousness thoughts: "Oh my gosh. They are all looking at me. Will I make it through this?"

This seared a visual and audio rendition into our psyche because it was so clever and perfectly demonstrated the meaning. I've become a better vocabulary teacher by allowing students the opportunity to demonstrate their thinking as a part of the instruction. I've used this trick of Steve's for years. Another trick I learned from that class was when Kelly, while teaching her word, tripped clumsily over the garbage can while telling us how graceful she was. You can bet I stole that demonstration of "dramatic irony."

Whether teaching vocabulary because domain-specific words are the key to success in your subject, or because you are a word nerd like myself, the approach that you take is crucial. I've heard teachers say, "Just bear with me. We have to get through the vocab definitions today." Hmmm. . . . Want to guess why students aren't falling all over themselves to learn these words? If you can't muster the enthusiasm to teach the word, you might not want to assess that word. If it is worth teaching, it is worth respecting, and if it is worth respecting, it is worth learning, not copying from the glossary.

Your Turn

Ready to give it a try? Here are some guiding questions:

- *Receptive and expressive vocabulary have different purposes.* How can you narrow down your list of vocabulary using this criteria?
- *Vocabulary work should be about words, not lists.* What can you do to eliminate the dreaded list?
- *Use visuals.* What technology could you use to create visual aids for your students?
- *Vocabulary integration is crucial.* Where can you "drop in" the vocabulary words to help students gain multiple methods of retrieval?
- *Tiered lists can take the guesswork out of vocab selection.* Which Tier is most important for your students to master?
- *Personalized Word Study taps emotional learning.* Is there a way to start a personalized word study in the near future?
- *Assessment can be differentiated.* Which method of assessing and tracking progress will work for you?

4

Project Based Learning

Differentiating Student Learning Experiences

I don't like to get hung up on names or labels for what happens in my classroom. However, when you join a chat on Twitter, it is common to introduce yourself with where you are from, what you teach, and a general philosophical statement. Essentially, it's your business card thrown into the ever-shifting winds of the Twittersphere. Recently, I found myself typing in my 140 characters: "Amber from Buffalo. NBCT. ELA8. Education blogger. PBL and Differentiation kinda girl." I smiled a little as I posted it because that just about sums it up, though it has taken over a decade to get that picture of who I am as a teacher just right.

Generally, I'm not very good at following the educational jargon, and I've found that those people who are inextricably bound to a particular phrase to describe their teaching aren't really about the teaching. You've heard all the labels: Project Based Learning. Inquiry Based Learning. Passion Projects. Problem Based Learning. For quite a while, I wasn't sure how to describe the learning experiences I was designing for my students, and honestly, I wasn't trying very hard to classify it. It doesn't matter what you call it either; rather, if you are creating an atmosphere of flexibility, where the learning of the individuals in your room matters more than the constraints of a label, then you know you are doing what is best for students. This chapter is a wide-angle view of Project Based Learning—my version of it—and it will provide you with a skeleton of your own that you can then flesh out to make it work for you, and you can call it whatever you'd like.

Sneak Peek

In this chapter, you will find ways to . . .

- *look at Project Based Learning, Problem Based Learning, and Passion Based Learning*
- *help your students find their BAM*
- *embrace the "we'll figure it out" attitude*
- *trust the process of immersion*
- *develop scaffolding*
- *manage time*
- *create a behavior management plan*
- *design organic mini-lessons*
- *examine types of presentations*
- *watch the learning environment change as you try out PBL (any of the PBLs!).*

What Does PBL Mean, Anyway?

John Larmer, editor in chief at the Buck Institute for Education, my go-to guide for all things Project Based Learning, describes the dilemma in his article "Project Based Learning vs. Problem Based Learning vs. XBL." He explains,

> We decided to think of Problem Based Learning as a subset of Project Based Learning; that is one of the ways a teacher could frame a project is "to solve a problem . . . The two PBLs are really two sides of the same coin. What type of PBL you decide to call your, er . . . *extended learning experience* just depends on how you frame it."
>
> (Larmer, 2013, p. 1)

It is up to you how you choose to picture and plan your projects. At the heart of this type of learning is an authenticity that you'll love to explore in your classroom.

BAM: There You Have It

The first time I introduce my students to an "extended learning experience," I simplify what we will do in Room 255. I explain that to be noticed, to be relevant, and to be successful in their world, they are going to need to know about what I call "BAM." They need to make a splash, create a stir, and bring their best selves to everything they do. They need to be constantly aware of what they are "putting out there" in the world because there's a paradoxical permanency in this age of constant change. Personality plays a large role in how you want to create a classroom culture ready for PBL. You will bring to it your own quirks, interests, and experiences—not to mention that every roster brings unique challenges and opportunities. The trick is to capitalize on how these factors can find synchronicity.

For me, when I tell them about Project Based Learning, I explain that BAM is what we are after:

> *Burning questions*: Gotta know, dying to know, really need to know, want to find out so much that you'll stay after school, talk about it at lunch, and text about it;
> *Authentic audiences*: Share with the world, publish it online, put it in a class blog, make a movie, call the newspaper, do whatever it takes to reach over 300 people (double your class size);
> *Millennial skills*: Make memes, create a gif, record a song, make a video game; essentially, this means posters won't cut it in the 21st century!

As you might have guessed, BAM is a good starting place, but students are going to need quite a bit more direction—or will they? I'm going to suggest that students will be best served if we act as facilitators. This is a new role for me because for most of my teaching career I viewed myself as the "knowledge giver." However, with the rise of the Internet, twenty-four-hour news cycles, social media, and smartphones, they literally have all the knowledge they could ever want at their fingertips. The trick is to inspire them to want to learn for themselves and show them the way. We need to illuminate the path with our experiences, and learn right beside them.

Modeling Academic Risk Taking

Modeling academic risk taking isn't always easy, and facilitating isn't something that comes naturally to me. It isn't my style to feel "unprepared." However, I'm starting to embrace this new role. For example, this year I started using Google Docs as my primary writing platform. My first impulse fifteen years ago would have been to learn everything there was to know about it, read several books about the best way to utilize it, create a curriculum, and then spend at least several days teaching it. I surprised myself this fall when my first impulse was "we'll figure it out." Until I began PBL, I just didn't know what students are capable of doing, but I know now that the best way for me to grow is to respect the learning curve and those who are much quicker than I am deciphering something new. An important step in embracing PBL is realizing that you are ceding control, not just to student curiosity, but to a non-linear learning experience. There are some of you who will be delighted to hand over some of the responsibility, but others will have to be more intentional about it (like me!).

I begin with a fall PBL project that is almost a rehearsal for the "real deal" of open opportunity that my students have with their spring project, which is a Passion Project, created entirely by each individual student.

The greatest challenge that I face in the fall each year is to convince students that they are able to think for themselves, find what they need to know, share it effectively, and take intellectual risks. They come to me, especially those high achieving students who want to please the teacher to earn the grade, without the ability to struggle. The students who find academics difficult sometimes seem to give up before they've started. I bet this happens in your classroom as well. I'm wondering if this is the deficit that so many people are talking about, but instead calling it a lack of grit. In my experience, once a student is deeply engaged, the ability to struggle kicks in; in my classroom, I try to create opportunities for students to become so wrapped up in something they are doing that they aren't remembering that they already worked on it for nine hours over the weekend.

The Goal Is Immersion!

I liken the immersion experience to gaming; Oliver, my seven-year-old, has just discovered Minecraft. At first, he didn't know what to do, so he spent a relatively short amount of time building, unable to "stay on task." This was not because he didn't like the game or have the desire to learn, but instead he felt powerless without some direction. I kept encouraging him to tell me what he was building and show me how he did it, creating a narrative to help give his experience context and show that it was worthy of his time. Did I know anything about Minecraft? Not a bit. But if we can help students orient themselves to a task and become invested in it, I think we can lead students to develop the confidence to stick to it when the "right" way isn't readily apparent. It wasn't too long until I had to bring Oliver back to the real world after he'd disappeared down the rabbit hole, creating games and roller coasters for hours.

In school, when my class is over and everyone else is filing out of the library, the stragglers are sometimes so immersed in their projects that we have to send them on their way. My teacher radar does not start picking up the "I have grit" signal emanating from my busy students, but instead, I get the "they're really into it" vibe, which is exactly what I hope for. Think about your own experiences of immersion and tap into that. What circumstances led to that feeling? Can you replicate that? What obstacles do you need to move for your students to reach this experience? For your first project, choose something that you feel comfortable with and you know you can talk about while answering a million questions. Remember, though, a million questions are better than none!

Fall Project: Creating a Utopia

Helping Students Find Their BAM
The first PBL project I do with my students is the culminating experience after we've read Lois Lowry's *The Giver*. Because this is the first time my students will have tried their hand at achieving BAM with their projects, it is more guided and scaffolded than their spring project, the Passion Project, which is easily adaptable to any subject. The Fishbowl discussion in chapter 2 lays the foundation for the first task and our future collective learning. The concepts introduced are meant to focus students and introduce some of the characteristics of a utopia, and these topics will continually spiral through our conversations as we read and discuss the novel.

Previewing the Project
It is really important to preview the project with students before they read the novel, because in order to create their own utopia, they will need to do their best to avoid negative unintended consequences such as those in the novel. I set their purpose for reading, and in this case, their burning question: What would make the "perfect" world? I introduce the project, and it actually is a great motivator in their reading as well.

Figure 4.1 Utopia Project

A utopia is a "perfect world." In the novel *The Giver*, you will see that the community is designed to have solved all the problems we face in our world; for example, there is no poverty, war, homelessness, drug addiction, or violence. Jonas lives in a utopian world designed to provide food, shelter, and safety to the people of the community. Now it is time to design your "perfect world." What would it look like? What would life be like for the people who live in your community? For your paper and project, you'll need to address each of the following topics. If there is a word or phrase bolded, you'll need to explain what it means. These are whole class vocabulary words.

BACKSTORY

In order for a utopian society to exist, there has had to be some inciting event that has caused the creation of a new society. Think of some of the **post-apocalyptic** books and movies that you know—*The Hunger Games*, *Mazerunner*, and *Divergent*. Consider the way those societies were formed. Decide upon a backstory for your community. You may make this a brief aspect of your work, or make it more involved if it concerns the way of life in your community.

MARKETABILITY

What is going to draw people to your community? Why would they want to live there? Why wouldn't they leave? You should look at this aspect of your community as an advertisement. Your project will include information about the following areas. Under each category, you must supply enough information to inform others of your community and entice them to join.

Government (approximately twelve sentences, in addition to the ten laws):

Every community needs laws, otherwise there would be chaos. Your laws may be based on a moral system, a political one, or something else. Some students like to have a theme for their community (**sustainability**, peace, friendship, etc.), and that will impact the way you govern your people and the laws you'd make.

- Create ten rules or laws in your community.
- Who makes the laws?
- How are the laws enforced? Is it a proactive approach or reactive?
- Is your community a **democracy**? A **dictatorship**? A **monarchy**? Something else?
- What happens when a person in the community breaks a law?

Family (approximately eight sentences):

- Are there families in your utopian community? If not, what replaces that structure?
- What are families going to be like in your community?

- Are the families going to be:

    Matriarchal: controlled by the mother of the family
    Patriarchal: controlled by the father of the family
    Equitable: neither matriarchal or patriarchal.

- How many kids should each family have? Is this *regulated*? Why or why not? If it is regulated, how?
- What are the living arrangements? Do families stick together or have freedom to move wherever they want?

Education (approximately ten sentences):

School is a way of preparing kids to be successful members of the community. Some people believe that school is the best way to **indoctrinate** young people to **conform** to the society.

- What will school be like in your community? It doesn't have to be traditional.
- What will be taught and what subjects will be required?
- How will education impact the community?
- How will schools in your community be different from the school you attend?

Housing (approximately eight sentences):

- Are there neighborhoods? Individual family dwellings?
- What are the neighborhoods like in your community?
- Do people live in separate houses? In townhouses? In apartments? In tents?
- Describe the dwellings in your community. Are all of the houses the same or different?
- Explain why you chose to design the houses and communities that way.

Employment (approximately thirty sentences; five per job and explanation):

Think about the jobs people must have to help your community function.

Choose five important jobs to describe. For each job, include at least five sentences describing:

- The title of the job
- The function of the job
- The type of people chosen for the job
- How people are chosen for the job
- How people are trained for the job

Include a picture of what a person employed in this job might look like (uniforms, etc.).

Money (approximately five sentences):

- Is there a system of money in your community?

If the answer is *yes*:

- Draw a picture of your money (coins and paper money).
- What is your money called?

If the answer is *no*:

- Why don't you have money?
- How do you "pay" people for their jobs?
- How do people get what they need to survive?

Transportation (approximately five sentences):

- How do people get around in your community?
- Is there a system of **mass transit**? Why or why not?

Environment/climate (approximately five sentences):

- Think about where you would have your community built.
- What is the climate like in your community? Tropical? Arctic? Do the seasons change?
- Are there animals in your community? What kinds? Are they pets or wild? Why?

Recreation (approximately five sentences):

- What is recreation like in your community?
- How much time do most people spend on recreation each week?
- What do people do for fun in your utopian community?
- Does the government control how people spend their free time?

Technology (approximately eight sentences):

- How does your community view technology?
- Are people technologically advanced? Do they live a more simple life?

ADDITIONAL REQUIREMENTS

- Name your community. BE CREATIVE!!!!!!
- Design a flag for your community. Think about color symbolism.
- Draw an overview map of your community. Make sure to label:
  - Houses
  - Schools
  - Business district (stores, etc.)
  - Roads
  - Government buildings
  - Areas for recreation
  - Any additional areas that are important for your community

When creating your utopian community, be creative and unique. The "perfect" society would only expect that . . . right???

CCSS.ELA-Literacy.W.8.3.c
Use a variety of transition words, phrases, and clauses to convey sequence, signal shifts from one time frame or setting to another, and show the relationships among experiences and events.

CCSS.ELA-Literacy.W.8.3.d
Use precise words and phrases, relevant descriptive details, and sensory language to capture the action and convey experiences and events.

CCSS.ELA-Literacy.W.8.4
Produce clear and coherent writing in which the development, organization, and style are appropriate to task, purpose, and audience.

CCSS.ELA-Literacy.W.8.5
With some guidance and support from peers and adults, develop and strengthen writing as needed by planning, revising, editing, rewriting, or trying a new approach, focusing on how well purpose and audience have been addressed. (Editing for conventions should demonstrate command of Language standards 1–3.)

CCSS.ELA-Literacy.W.8.6
Use technology, including the Internet, to produce and publish writing and present the relationships between information and ideas efficiently as well as to interact and collaborate with others.

CCSS.ELA-Literacy.W.8.7
Conduct short research projects to answer a question (including a self-generated question), drawing on several sources and generating additional related, focused questions that allow for multiple avenues of exploration.

CCSS.ELA-Literacy.SL.8.4
Present claims and findings, emphasizing salient points in a focused, coherent manner with relevant evidence, sound valid reasoning, and well-chosen details; use appropriate eye contact, adequate volume, and clear pronunciation.

CCSS.ELA-Literacy.SL.8.5
Integrate multimedia and visual displays into presentations to clarify information, strengthen claims and evidence, and add interest.

CCSS.ELA-Literacy.SL.8.6
Adapt speech to a variety of contexts and tasks, demonstrating command of formal English when indicated or appropriate.

As they read the novel and encounter the methods by which the community achieves its version of the perfect world, they are also thinking about how their committee will create a utopia. For example, one of the topics we discuss is that in a perfect world, people will feel valued, and not languish in pain and depression in their old age. Sounds honorable enough, right? Well, if you haven't read the novel, I won't ruin it for you, but I will say this, people do lots of things that don't seem so moral in the light of day, in the name of doing what's best for another group of people. What topics do you cover that will lend themselves to great discussions?

Give the Project the Time It Deserves

After the students complete the book, they are given five in-class workdays. To some teachers, this may seem like a deal breaker. How can I "give up" this much time? Don't I have things I need to teach? The fact is, I don't have things to teach at this point, as I've guided them through the novel; rather, they have things to discover and learn *on their own*. I'm not giving up anything, but instead I'm giving them what they need: time to think, collaborate, research, and create with the guidance of trusted facilitators (in my case, this means me, the librarian, two Special Education teachers, and an English as a New Language [ENL] teacher). Additionally, it means that they have time to learn from each other. It is very common for me to get everyone's attention, then ask the question, "Can someone show Tom how to put the map in his document?" and find that students are more than happy to help each other out. Instead of my being that "giver of knowledge," I'm now operating as the obstacle mover and bringing students together to learn from each other—much like we all learn in "real life."

Create an Intentional Learning Environment (In Other Words, Behave!)

If you are imagining that this is a bit messy and loud, you'd be correct. I tend to look at it this way: Chatter and motion will always be better than cookie cutter compliance. Sure, that cookie cutter compliance might look like you have great classroom management, but it can also mean that you *only* have great classroom management, as compliance does not equate to learning. I have very specific tools and mantras that I use from day one to allow the "tight but loose" behavior system to work its magic. In a project based classroom, parameters have to be set so that students know how to move within them. This "training" begins immediately because by the time we start our fall PBL project, they need to be on board with our class culture. Here are the guidelines I have for my students (which I explicitly teach, much like Harry Wong's *First Days of School*):

> *We must be able to get the entire class's attention immediately.*
>
> > I'll clap, and you'll stop what you are doing, clap back, stop what you are doing and look at me. If you need to ask a

question or make a comment that the entire class needs to hear, use this method, and we'll stop and give you our full attention. Also, when you are standing in front of the class, get their attention before you begin presenting by clapping.

I have to trust you to move around the building, going only where you are supposed to, and representing our class as independent and important students at work. This building is full of resources, and we need to take advantage of their knowledge.

Abuse it, and you'll lose it. If it is ever reported that you are disruptive, distracting, or disrespectful, you will have shown me that you need more structure and will not be permitted to leave my supervision.

I have to believe you have good judgment regarding technology. If you ask to use your device, I'm going to say yes (if your parents agree on the technology release form). I'm assuming that you need to look something up, edit a Google Doc, tweak your PowerPoint, or research. I'm assuming you are taking notes or working towards our goal.

If you can't handle the responsibility, freedom is restricted. You'll need to use technology, of course, but you'll need to limit that to school computers, which are monitored.

I need you to understand that you are all my kiddos. Everyone must be treated with respect. If someone isn't good at something, we help. If someone is good at something, we share. This way of learning isn't about grading; it is about growing. You need each other, and the sooner you learn that, the more effective you'll be. Use your talents and help others use theirs.

I know you don't have to be friends with everyone. I respect that. However, common courtesy is required, no matter your personal opinions. In real life, there are always people you don't want to work with, but in real life, one of those people could be your boss.

This type of learning is about the individual because you are all different. If you have a question about what I've asked another student to do that is different than what you are doing, ask me. I'll explain to you the learning goal, which may be met in a variety of ways. It's my job to help all of you reach your potential, and that does not always mean sameness.

> Remember, unless the learning goal is writing an essay, then you don't all have to write an essay. If you have an idea about how you'd like me to assess you, tell me. I'm always open to your ideas about "showing what you know."

Maybe this sounds a whole lot like the hippie young teacher from my first days of teaching. There's a difference, though: I used to want this type of atmosphere for learning because it made *me* feel comfortable. Nowadays, I know that differentiation works, so this isn't a suggestion or a philosophy, but instead an *intentional learning environment*. Do I feel like an idiot the first time I clap at 8th graders who stare with disbelief, as if they had been transported back to 1st grade? You bet. Do I know that the world is more complex than the classroom culture I'm attempting to establish? Sure. But, the first time we are working, and the class is too loud, and a student claps, and we all clap back, and look expectantly at a student who asks, "Does anyone know how to insert a video into a Prezi?" I am so proud to be a part of what has been created, because there's something magical when a 13-year-old takes charge of his education.

During the project's five workdays, students are meeting with the committees they have formed. Not all students will choose to work in a group, but those who do need to come up with a plan of action to distribute the workload.

Figure 4.2 Planning and Reflection Guide for *The Giver* Project

Fill in Part 1, with your committee, BEFORE you begin. Each committee member will need to hand in one:

Your Name: _____ ELA Period: _____
Names of Other Group Members: _____

PART 1:

Put a check in front of the parts of the project you will be working on:

_____ Government   _____ Education   _____ Family
_____ Housing   _____ Employment   _____ Money

_____ Transportation	_____ Environment/Climate	_____ Recreation
_____ Technology	_____ Name of Community	_____ Flag
_____ Map	_____ Writing the Paper	_____ Presentation Prep
_____ Lead Presenter*	_____ Tech Coordinator**	_____ Liaison***

*Lead Presenter: Introduces the committee, welcomes visitors, and gives an overview for visitors of the work we've been doing.

**Tech Coordinator: Responsible for making sure that the project is sent to the teacher or shared via Google. Also, has a backup on a jump drive. This person has double-checked all of the slides for spelling and accuracy.

***Liaison: This person will communicate with the teacher when there is a question or a request. This saves five people from asking the same question.

Common study hall, after school time, or ability to work digitally (explain how you and your group will collaborate). If you are working alone, jot down some of your work times:

_____
_____
_____

PART 2:

Grade You'd Give Yourself: _____
Justification and Rationale:

_____
_____

Reflections About Your Group:

_____
_____

Next Time:

_____
_____

This is an important step, because later I'll have them do a final reflection that brings them full circle and allows them to plan for their next project. After they've established their roles and responsibilities, I check in, step back, and let them have some space. I find a central location, sit down, and let them work. I try very hard not to interfere because they need to have the creative space to take risks when they build their utopia. If I'm breathing down their necks, I may dissuade them from creating a community that I don't explicitly approve of, one that they may be able to imagine, but I can't. For example, one of the best projects of the year is well beyond my imagination, but allowed some of my more science-minded guys to explore their ideas.

Figure 4.3 Introduction to the H2Dome Community

The H2Dome Community commenced in the year 3033 after technology became too advanced for the human race. Technological equipment throughout the world began communicating with each other. Sensitive government equipment was compromised, nuclear warheads and hydrogen bombs were activated, creating world-wide catastrophic destruction. 7.5 million survivors came out of many nuclear bomb shelters and descended 28,000 feet below the surface of the Atlantic ocean off the coast of what used to be called Puerto Rico, now called "The Zone". "The Zone" is a dangerous place where mutated animals constantly try to terminate humans. The Surface is visited regularly to gather mutated fruits and vegetables and bring back meat of the mutated animals killed. There are 9 domes 8 residential/recreational domes and one massive government dome.

    The Government Dome has everything the residential domes has but better community areas and special sports arenas. Entrances to each dome are on the water surface, tubes plunge 28,000 feet exceeding speeds of 50 mph eventually reaching the community. The H2Dome community is thriving due to amazingly advanced, under-control, technology and the hunters-gatherers who risk their lives to travel to the surface in search of food. New plants are discovered every day, and in the agricultural dome they are duplicated to help maintain and grow our abundant resources. The people in all communities are mutated to be able to survive in areas with high levels of radiation, in high pressure situations, and can breathe under water. Some mutations have their drawbacks, such as many people are born with a dorsal fin or webbed feet, but these are surgically removed at 2 months of age since there are no real benefits to them.
    (Introduction to the underwater-based H2Dome Community, a utopia created by Jakob Nye, Ben Egloff, Parker Colling, and Harrison Drozen)

Teach Them What They Need to Know (and They All Need Commas)

I begin each of these five days with a mini-lesson that I create based on student needs. For example, I noticed that many students were using an online map creator, but it wouldn't allow them to save their map as an attachment. I asked students to think about this problem and let me know if they solve it. Within a few minutes, one of my students came over and explained that a great work-around was just to take a screen shot and then drop it into the paper and the presentation. She explained to me what to do (hold down the Command, Shift, and 4 keys). I learned from her, and the next day that's how I started class. Then I was able to share that she taught me how to do it, and to send students her way if they still need help.

Presentation Logistics: It Takes Longer Than You Think

As students begin to finish their papers, they create their presentation. Students work at different paces and with varying levels of commitment, so I stagger the presentations based on my observations. However, I also want to consider when they will have the biggest audience, so I email all parents and family members an invitation. I ask them to let me know ASAP if they can make it, and I then assign students to that date. Even as some students are still working on the paper, I lay out the expectations of the presentation so that those ready to move on can do so.

Figure 4.4 Presentation Tips

Requirements:

- A PowerPoint, Prezi, Haiku Deck, Google Slides presentation, or some other presentation tool;
- Equal participation by committee members;
- You should be ready to present on any day (have jump drive ready or the ability to retrieve online);
- Include each category from your paper; this should take approximately ten minutes.

What Good Presenters Do:

- Project your voice so that everyone hears.
- Never turn your back to the crowd (especially to read the screen).
- Exude enthusiasm.
- Anticipate questions (and answer them in your presentation).
- Use notecards instead of reading from the screen.

What Great Presenters Do:

- Make eye contact with a variety of people in the crowd (scanning).
- Project your voice so that everyone hears and use your voice to accentuate a point or demonstrate the importance of something (use different tones and cadences).
- Include minimal text and bullets, uses visuals and knows what to say without reading at all (this takes practice!).
- Create an enthusiastic atmosphere.
- Anticipate and answer questions and leave the audience with a desire to learn more.
- Use the presentation tool as an assessor, not a crutch.

The Big No-No's:

- Never write paragraphs on a slide. Ever.
- Don't use fonts that can't be read by everyone in the last row.
- Don't use backgrounds that are pictures UNLESS you make them transparent.
- Never present without practice.
- Don't use words that you can't pronounce easily (names could be an exception).
- Don't look at me when you are presenting.
- Don't go over or under two minutes of the expected presentation time.

Give students an additional week before presentations begin. The biggest rookie mistake I ever made was forcing the presentations to start when I wanted, not when the students had created a utopia they'd be proud of. Don't let the logistics get in the way of learning. In the week in between, I sometimes do some stand-alone lessons that I design based on what I'm seeing in the papers as they are coming in. I allow students a rolling submission window so that I'm not swamped with grading; however, they must have their paper in before the last day of presentations. Most students want to get their papers in right away so that they can get immediate feedback. Generally, I can count on teaching students how to combine sentences, how to use commas, and how to use vivid verbs and sensory adjectives. I try to pull positive examples from students' papers, but I have these lessons prepped and ready to go.

Occasionally, I'll spend a few days watching the movie version with my students, and I allow those who need more time to obtain passes to work in the library or with their Special Education teachers. I don't require this, but I do want to give them options. They should not be punished for not working as quickly as others, but they might want the extra time or attention. In the case of *The Giver*, the movie is a great comparison piece, per CCSS:

> **CCSS.ELA-Literacy.RL.8.7**
> Analyze the extent to which a filmed or live production of a story or drama stays faithful to or departs from the text or script, evaluating the choices made by the director or actors.

Students have become immersed in their papers and projects, so the presentation days are very exciting. Parents, teachers, administrators, and even students' friends come to Room 255 to see the utopias that we've created. My role on these days is to welcome our guests and make sure I'm providing quality feedback to the presenters. The "lead presenter" in each group is tasked with introducing the committee members and briefly explaining to our guests what our project entails. I sit in the back with my pile of rubrics, and scribble furiously. I use the Buck Institute for Education Common Core Aligned PBL Presentation Rubric because it is thorough, easy to use, and objective.

Figure 4.5 Presentation Rubric for PBL (for Grades 6–8; Common Core ELA Aligned)

	Below Standard	Approaching Standard	At Standard	Above Standard ✓
Explanation of Ideas & Information	◆ uses too few, inappropriate, or irrelevant descriptions, facts, details, or examples to support ideas	◆ uses some descriptions, facts, details, and examples that support ideas, but there may not be enough, or some are irrelevant	◆ uses relevant, well-chosen descriptions, facts, details, and examples to support claims, findings, arguments, or an answer to a Driving Question (CC 6–8.SL.4)	
Organization	◆ does not include important parts required in the presentation ◆ does not have a main idea or presents ideas in an order that does not make sense ◆ does not have an introduction and/or conclusion ◆ uses time poorly; the whole presentation, or a part of it, is too short or too long	◆ includes almost everything required in the presentation ◆ moves from one idea to the next, but main idea may not be clear or some ideas may be in the wrong order ◆ has an introduction and conclusion, but they are not effective ◆ generally times presentation well, but may spend too much or too little time on a topic, audio/visual aid, or idea	◆ includes everything required in the presentation ◆ states main idea and moves from one idea to the next in a logical order, emphasizing main points in a focused, coherent manner (CC 6–8.SL.4) ◆ has an effective introduction and conclusion ◆ organizes time well; no part of the presentation is rushed, too short or too long	
Eyes & Body	◆ does not look at audience; reads notes or slides ◆ does not use gestures or movements ◆ lacks poise and confidence (fidgets, slouches, appears nervous) ◆ wears clothing inappropriate for the occasion	◆ makes infrequent eye contact; reads notes or slides most of the time ◆ uses a few gestures or movements but they do not look natural ◆ shows some poise and confidence (only a little fidgeting or nervous movement) ◆ makes some attempt to wear clothing appropriate for the occasion	◆ keeps eye contact with audience most of the time; only glances at notes or slides (CC 6–8.SL.4) ◆ uses natural gestures and movements ◆ looks poised and confident ◆ wears clothing appropriate for the occasion	

Voice	◆ mumbles or speaks too quickly or slowly ◆ speaks too softly to be understood ◆ frequently uses "filler" words ("uh, um, so, and, like, etc.") ◆ does not speak appropriately for the context and task (may be too informal, use slang)	◆ speaks clearly most of the time; sometimes too quickly or slowly ◆ speaks loudly enough for most of the audience to hear, but may speak in a monotone ◆ occasionally uses filler words ◆ tries to speak appropriately for the context and task	◆ speaks clearly; not too quickly or slowly (CC 6–8.SL.4) ◆ speaks loudly enough for everyone to hear; changes tone to maintain interest (CC 6–8.SL.4) ◆ rarely uses filler words ◆ speaks appropriately for the context and task, demonstrating command of formal English when appropriate (CC 6–8.SL.6)
Presentation Aids	◆ does not use audio/visual aids or media ◆ attempts to use one or a few audio/visual aids or media but they distract from or do not add to the presentation	◆ uses audio/visual aids or media, but they sometimes distract from or do not add to the presentation	◆ uses well-produced audio/visual aids or media to clarify information, emphasize important points, strengthen arguments, and add interest (CC 6–8.SL.5)
Response to Audience Questions	◆ does not address audience questions (goes off topic or misunderstands without seeking clarification)	◆ answers some audience questions, but not always clearly or completely	◆ answers audience questions clearly and completely ◆ seeks clarification, admits "I don't know," or explains how the answer might be found when unable to answer a question
Participation in Team Presentations	◆ not all team members participate; only one or two speak	◆ all team members participate, but not equally	◆ all team members participate for about the same length of time ◆ all team members are able to answer questions about the topic as a whole, not just their part of it

And, even though it is not a part of their grade, I like how the rubric has a section where I can assess their ability to work together as a team.

Does this project meet the criteria for Project Based Learning or one of the other labels? I think so, yes, but I also don't really worry too much about those types of questions. If I do, I could become like my son as he began playing Minecraft—too paralyzed by what I'm supposed to be doing to do anything. Just as I helped him find his story, I think that is the key for all of us. *My* version here may not be *your* best chance at creating an engaged classroom, as you may have obstacles that I can't even imagine. But, if you forge ahead, building what you need, I believe that you'll find the uncertainty will be worth the learning experiences you build for your students. And, when you feel ready, there's always the Passion Project to do!

Spring Project: Finding Your Passion

Putting Their BAM in Action to Find Their Passion Project

Project Based Learning must meet the needs of your individual classroom to be successful. I invented the "Passion Project" out of necessity. April in New York is one of the most frustrating times to be a teacher. There are three days of ELA assessments and an additional three days of Math assessments, creating alternate schedules, make-ups, sub shortages, and a general exhaustion among students and staff. In my particular situation, we also score our assessments locally, so that means I will be out on a Monday/Tuesday for two weeks in a row. Did I mention that in most years we also have our spring break thrown into the mix? There are some Aprils when I see my students for a "regular" instruction day only four or five times.

In the midst of this exhausting month, how can I instruct my students, particularly if I don't see them in a regular, predictable way? As it turns out, I really can't, but if I have trained them well with the Utopia Project, and continued to instill confidence and independence, then April can actually be a great learning opportunity. I'm proud to say that April is now one of my students' favorite times of year because they are rewarded with the freedom to pursue an individual interest—thus, the Passion Project.

Figure 4.6 Passion Project

When you were little, did you ask a million questions about dinosaurs, space, germs, or some other topic, but no one really answered your questions? Ever wonder about something late into the night? Is there a burning question, searing your brain? If so, you are going to love this project. If not, then we're going to open your mind to new possibilities!

You are going to find your passion—something you want to read about, write about, take pictures of, share a story about, and even make a website to share your passion.

How It Works

First, we'll do some activities to help those who don't have a topic yet. You'll want to keep in mind that this is an individual project, and we'll be working on it for about a month and a half.

Next, after you have a topic, we'll formulate a "burning question." We'll do the "Igniting the Burning Question" activity to help you figure this out. A burning question is something that you want to solve, discover, explore, or seek during your Passion Project journey. This question should be at the center of all you do. Your website will be designed to share the "answer" to your question. Don't worry . . . some questions lead to more questions, but you'll want to consider this carefully. You'll need to run it by me, since this part is such a big deal.

After you have a topic and a burning question, then you're going to find a non-fiction book on the topic. It has to be a *book*. I know . . . I know . . . there's this thing called the Internet. Don't worry, you'll get to that. First though, you are going to read a book to gather background knowledge before your project really starts to take shape. When should you read this book? As soon as possible. You'll have reading time during class in the early part of the month, but you should carry this book with you to also read during study halls and free times.

Then, after you've read your book, the real fun begins! You'll need to design your "Project Parameters." A parameter is a rule or limit that controls what something is or how it should be done. Most of the time, I give you the parameters, but the beauty of this project is to find ways to chase your passion, and then, of course, "show what you know." I've italicized every graded part of the project (classwork or quiz grades).

Here's our timeline, starting with the very first steps:

> **March 28**: Library to get book (get it ahead of time if you want). *Topic and burning question should be firmed up and approved.*
> **March 29–30**: Creating "Project Parameters" in class. Must be handed in on March 31. (These parameters will be listed on your website.)
> **March 31**: You will be learning how to make the website.
> **April 4**: Class check-in day—*share Project Parameters with Resource Group.*
> **April 5–7**: ELA ASSESSMENTS (*Class schedules will be different, and I may not see you for class time. Continue on with your reading. This project is NOT dependent on coming to class.)
> **April 8**: Revisiting burning questions.

April 11–12: *Conferencing* with me.
April 13–15: MATH ASSESSMENTS (*Class schedules will be different, and I may not see you for class time. Continue on with your reading. This project is NOT dependent on coming to class.)
April 18–19: (I will be out scoring assessments.) Continue reading.
April 20: Checkpoint. What progress have you made towards your project? Meet with Resource Group to debrief and strategize. Bring in evidence of what you have been doing.
April 21: Explanation of requirements for webpage; receive "Webpage Guidelines."
April 22: Q and A of website and review the basics.
April 25–26: (I will be out scoring assessments.) Finish reading. Book should be complete by April 27.
April 27: Learning how to write a book review.
April 28–29: Writing the "Book Review" (This will appear on your website).
May 2–4: Website workdays.
May 5: Explanation of "Process Presentation."
May 6: Presentation planning.
May 9: Presentation workday.
May 10–13: Presentations (*must be 5–7 minutes).
May 16–17: Presentations.
May 18: Debriefing and Reflection.

FAQ (Frequently Asked Questions)

- How am I supposed to do this if I don't have the Internet at home?

  - Work in study halls.
  - Stay after school.
  - We'll be working on this a substantial amount during class.

- What if I don't know how to build a website?

  - I'll help.
  - Your friends will help.
  - The librarian will help.
  - Watch the tutorials.

- Why are the presentations timed?

  - Believe it or not, shorter presentations require more skill.
  - We have lots of students.
  - You have mastered the basics (loud, clear, prepared), so it is time to push ahead.

- What is a Process Presentation?

  - It is the narrative of your journey.
  - It will be told using the website you build.
  - It is personal.

- Can I invite people to the presentation?

  - Yes, of course!
  - I will be inviting your parents and our administrators.

- What happens if I am not taking the assessments?
  - You'll have even more time on the project.
- What happens if I am taking the assessments?
  - You'll read when you have completed the assessment.
- Can I do the same project as someone else?
  - Yes and No.
  - Yes: You may have the same topic and even the same question.
  - No: You are not creating a collaborative project, but you are encouraged to help each other out.
- Do I have to use Wix?
  - No. It is just very easy to use, and I can give you the most guidance.
- What if my parents don't want me to create a webpage?
  - You may do a Prezi.
  - Please realize that we will keep these websites set to private, so have your parents talk to me if there are any concerns.

The first thing you'll notice is that the Passion Project is for individuals, not groups. That is simply the solution to a logistical nightmare. This project can easily be adjusted to allow groups who share similar interests to work together. Also, this project is extremely easy to adapt to all domains, as long as you are willing to stretch the parameters of what you typically consider "yours" in the curriculum. This learning experience takes about a month and a half, including the presentations. I've included the dates so that you can sense the pacing and ways I've had to adjust to scheduling issues. Let me be the first to say that my initial response to the craziness of April was to assign a book, leave questions to go with the chapters, and give a quiz each week. Let me also say that my students were miserable, I had acquired a ton of grading that offered zero meaningful feedback to my students, and I had to face a bunch of frustrated parents whose children weren't keeping up with all the busy work. I apologized profusely to that first class who lived it, but I didn't know then that there was an alternative.

Designing the Learning Experiences

The Passion Project is student-driven research with three learning experiences designed by the individual student. The first step is to guide students through the process of organizing themselves by helping them ignite the burning question.

Figure 4.7 Igniting the Burning Question

You are going to need a question that drives the project. This is best understood through examples. First, you'll see the broad topic. Then, you'll have a list of burning questions that could become a project. Remember, you aren't doing a report. You are designing a learning experience and then showing what you learned via the website. Each burning question lists several possible activities that you could do as you design your Project Parameters. Your project will only focus on one burning question, but must consist of three activities. (This does not include the Project Parameters and Book Review that will be on the website. This means there will be a total of five buttons or categories.)

- ◆ Gaming
  - Are video games to blame for an increasingly violent society? (Are we more violent?)
    - Research if we are more violent or not.
    - Find out about the rating system and create an alternate one.
    - Play video games and journal the experience. (What's the appeal?)
    - Create a survey (Survey Monkey is easy and free for ten questions) that gathers data about gaming habits. Share the results in charts, graphs, and so on.
    - Write a speech (record yourself giving it to put on the website).
    - Design your own game.
    - Talk to serious gamers.
    - Create a montage of video game footage to prove or disprove that video games make society more violent.
  - Why are video games more appealing to boys? (Is there a gender bias?)
    - Research if gaming is more appealing to boys.
    - Find out and analyze how games are marketed.
    - Create a survey (Survey Monkey is easy and free for ten questions) that gathers data about gaming habits. Share the results in charts, graphs, and so on.
    - Write a speech (record yourself giving it to put on the website).
    - Design your own game.
    - Talk to a game designer about gender bias (email is OK).
    - Gather biased commercials into a montage.
  - How can gaming simulations be used for job training?
    - Research eye/hand coordination.
    - Learn about simulations.
    - Find out what jobs are improved by simulations.
    - Find out the limitations of simulations.
    - Analyze the role of simulations in terrorism.
    - Look at the medical field and research methods doctors use.
  - How do I become a game designer? Is it a good job?
    - Research colleges with game design programs.
    - Contact a designer and ask for his/her advice.

- Fill out a college application as if you were actually applying.
- Design your own game.
- Trace the history of game design.
- Find out the average salary for a first-year game designer, then create a budget for all of your living expenses using that number.

♦ Fashion

- Why are clothes so expensive?
    - Research sweat shops (overseas).
    - Is there a bias—do companies only want certain kinds of people (rich ones) wearing their clothes? (Look up Tommy Hilfiger on that one.)
    - What is the actual cost of making an item of clothing? Do some comparing with charts, graphs, and so on.
    - Compare boy versus girl clothing.
    - What does "licensing" mean?
- How does a designer come out with a new line?
    - Research a new designer.
    - Contact (via email) a designer to ask about his/her inspiration.
    - Design a few items of clothing.
    - Make an item of clothing.
    - Sketch what inspires you and turn that into a theme for a line of clothes.
- Is a designer a good job? How do you become one?
    - Research colleges with fashion design programs.
    - Contact a designer and ask for his/her advice.
    - Fill out a college application as if you were actually applying.
    - Design a few items of clothing.
    - Trace the history of clothing.
    - Find out the average salary for a first-year designer, then create a budget for all of your living expenses using that number.
- Do styles change or actually repeat themselves?
    - Research fashion.
    - Read new and old fashion magazines, and notice trends.
    - Critique a few designers and see if they recycle ideas.
    - Create a visual compare/contrast (2016 with 1986 would be good).
    - Who are the trendsetters? Why?
    - How does social media impact fashion?

These are examples meant to give you some idea of the type of projects you can do. I'm sure you'll come up with some really amazing learning experiences to explore your passion!

This is a chance for me to demonstrate my thinking as I explain the multiple burning questions I've modeled. It is important for students to understand that burning questions are very personal, based on the knowledge they already have about the topic, and can lead their project down very different paths. Students are in their Resource Groups and are able to run their ideas by their peers in a non-threatening way.

Once they know what they are trying to learn, they will need to read a non-fiction book to develop some background knowledge before they absolutely nail down what their burning question will be. Sometimes students will know so little about the topic they are researching that at first they don't have the understanding to know what they don't know. This early reading will form the rest of the project, so I enlist the help of the librarian, Special Education teachers, and the ENL (English as a New Language) teacher to help students locate an appropriate book. The first question everyone wants to know is "How many pages?" but that is not a set number. For example, if a student's burning question is "How Will the World End?" and that child chooses to read a science-heavy book, I'd expect fewer pages because of the difficult topic. On the other hand, if a student wants to know "What is the best breed of dog for families?" I'm going to expect a little more reading on the topic because ostensibly what they are reading will require less heavy lifting than the science text.

Because students know me well by the end of the year, there will be students who will want to replace reading a book with reading several magazine or Internet articles. As long as it is non-fiction and they read an equitable number of pages, I let them explore in the direction they want to go. I require that they do an annotated bibliography instead of the Book Review.

Figure 4.8 Book Review

After you've finished reading your book, you'll need to do a book review for your website. Book reviews generally follow a pretty specific pattern. Here are some guidelines:

- Include the title (italicized), author, publisher, and date of publication.
- Describe the way the book is organized (chapters, sections, parts, etc.).
    - Is this an effective way for the book to be organized?
    - If there are any special features (maps, pictures, tables, charts), describe them.
    - Is there an index, glossary, footnotes, or other added parts? Are they helpful?

- Write a brief summary of the book.
  - What are some of the specific sections in the book that were most helpful and/or interesting?
  - Describe why this book was appealing to you.
- What is the main claim of the book?
- What is the author's purpose for writing it?
- Determine why we should listen to this author about the topic—what are his/her credentials or experiences that make him/her an expert?
- Who would like this book?

Read several book reviews before you begin so that you'll understand the tone this type of writing takes. You don't want it to sound like an elementary school book report, but you'll also want to give your opinion.

The review should be about 250–350 words. Find pictures to go along with the review. Create a tab or button for the review on your website. Include a link to the book's webpage or author's site.

One of the caveats, though, is that students have to find out how to do an annotated bibliography on their own, but by this point, I've taught them how to locate what they need to know on the Internet. It isn't that I am lazy or don't want to teach an annotated bibliography, but instead I seek to teach them an important lesson. If you are going to ever ask to do something different or meet requirements in your own way, you'll need to carry the burden of that yourself.

The Book Review

However, I do provide a model for students of the Book Review assignment, as they very well may have never read one. The reason I add this requirement is to add a level of accountability, particularly since I won't be there to supervise. Additionally, there is value in exposing them to new types of writing. My example is a pretty typical book review, and I can share the process by which I wrote it, giving students insights into my writing process, and validating the types of problems they will run into.

Figure 4.9 Pedagogy Should Always Precede Technology: SAS Curriculum Pathways *Mobile Learning*

Originally published on GettingSmart.com
November 18, 2015
By Amber Chandler

Full disclaimer: I am a teacher, and I want to keep my job. When people talk about programs to replace face-to-face teaching and learning experiences (my classroom!), I start to squirm. I started *Mobile Learning*, a book written collaboratively by SAS Curriculum Pathways, with a healthy dose of skepticism; however, I was soon won over because there is a respectful balance between the promotion of mobile learning and the necessity for sound pedagogy.

In fact, even as the authors discuss the incomprehensible one million apps available on Apple's App Store, they also warn that just because "there's an app for that" doesn't mean that young learners are equipped to make educational decisions alone. In fact, they admonish, "while the proliferation of apps might tempt one to scour the app store in search of the perfect app, pedagogy should always precede technology or, in this case, pedagogy should always be the primary consideration, rather than focusing only of the content of the app." Clearly, it didn't take me long to start trusting the authors. It was on page 59, just in case you're curious.

It seems every institution, be it a middle school or a university, includes the phrase "lifelong learner" in their vision statement or motto. What everyone is getting at, I think, is the collective wish of educators to ignite a spark that can't be put out. The authors though, suggest a 2.0 version of this wish, one that meets the needs of Digital Natives: They believe that mobile learning blurs the lines between formal and informal learning, in essence, facilitating the journey of the lifelong learner. Just as a master teacher is the channel for discovery, mobile devices are a portable conduit for all-the-time learning.

However, educators who wish to create a mobile classroom must recognize and extinguish desires to integrate technology piecemeal and without thoughtful consideration. The authors advise that "successful integrations of mobile devices does not mean retrofitting existing lessons but, instead, redefining them in terms of student participation and scope." *Mobile Learning* is the manual for this important evolution in education. At the core, the book tackles the underlying hotbed political question in education: Are schools preparing students for the real world? The authors contend that the answer is that most schools don't, but are optimistic that schools can.

The authors spend most of the book providing an inside look into the mobile and app world that most readers will find both interesting and mind-boggling. Until I read this book, I considered myself pretty current. Now I know that unless you make a concerted and concentrated effort, you won't be current—there's so much happening, so fast, that knowing the fundamental attributes is really important. The "Mobile Technology's Defining Features" chapter was by far the most useful. If you've ever felt like a dinosaur because a kid who was born the same year you graduated college is throwing words at you like weapons of superiority, then this chapter will be very enlightening. It isn't that you haven't heard of 3G connectivity, operating systems, the cloud, or push notifications, but after reading this book you'll know enough to have a conversation instead of standing there, nodding, trying not to give away that you don't speak the language like a native.

The book also made me want to pursue a new career in educational app development. As an educator, I was fascinated by the complexity of this process and intrigued by the layers of analysis that occur to ensure the best app with the most user-friendly experience. As an English teacher, I loved reading about what the authors call "User Interface Metaphors." For example, the outline of a house is easy enough for readers to relate to, indicating a move back to the home screen. However, developers must truly know and understand their audiences in order to create icons or interface options that make sense and are familiar to their users. Learning about these design elements has piqued my interest in apps, as choosing appropriate apps is now a more thoughtful process because I am now well-informed.

It is a testament to the authors' sound writing that I found entire chapters that aren't directly applicable to my life—"Apps for Preschoolers," for example—to be very interesting and engaging. The authors have a wonderful voice for informing the reader but continually deferring to us as well. Instead of a list of directives or an implied conceit, it is with a nod to the reader that the authors explain, "It's incumbent on parents to determine the value of these technologies for children. Passback or hold back? Should we treat mobile apps as junk food or nutritious vegetables?" Although the authors surely have their own opinions, it never feels condescending, but rather the new information empowers consumers.

The last time a book made me feel both newly informed and entirely inadequate (but in a good way!), was Thomas Friedman's *The World Is Flat*. When systems are broken down, industries illuminated, and a new way of looking at human relationships is introduced, it is to be expected that the ground doesn't seem as solid. However, having read the book, I feel prepared that if I need to know more or learn more, I'll know where to turn—to the staggeringly complex, yet enticingly approachable world of mobile learning.

Creating the Project Parameters

Next, students will need to set Project Parameters.

Figure 4.10 Passion Project Parameters

Topic: _____
Burning question: _____

The book I am reading is: _____
It is written by: _____
There are _____ pages.

Your website must include a summary of this sheet and the Book Review.

The website will highlight the three activities that you design. Explain in each space exactly what you are planning on doing.

Activity #1: _____ Deadline: _____
_____

How will we know if you were successful or not?
_____
_____

Activity #2: _____ Deadline: _____
_____

How will we know if you were successful or not?
_____
_____

Activity #3: _____ Deadline: _____
_____

How will we know if you were successful or not?
_____
_____

This will help students understand the scope and sequence of what they want to do. I've given them the example learning experiences when we talk about forming the burning question, and this is when they formulate what they will do. This is the most exciting part for them and me. The activities they create are as unique as they are, showcasing their unique skills and talents, as well as allowing students to work at different paces. Differentiation such as this allows all students to do challenging and meaningful work while demonstrating the skills I've set out to assess. In this case, the project is designed to provide learning experiences that meet the following College and Career Anchor Standards:

> **CCSS.ELA-Literacy.CCRA.R.1**
> Read closely to determine what the text says explicitly and to make logical inferences from it; cite specific textual evidence when writing or speaking to support conclusions drawn from the text.

CCSS.ELA-Literacy.CCRA.R.2

Determine central ideas or themes of a text and analyze their development; summarize the key supporting details and ideas.

CCSS.ELA-Literacy.CCRA.R.10

Read and comprehend complex literary and informational texts independently and proficiently.

CCSS.ELA-Literacy.CCRA.W.2

Write informative/explanatory texts to examine and convey complex ideas and information clearly and accurately through the effective selection, organization, and analysis of content.

CCSS.ELA-Literacy.CCRA.W.4

Produce clear and coherent writing in which the development, organization, and style are appropriate to task, purpose, and audience.

CCSS.ELA-Literacy.CCRA.W.6

Use technology, including the Internet, to produce and publish writing and to interact and collaborate with others.

CCSS.ELA-Literacy.CCRA.W.7

Conduct short as well as more sustained research projects based on focused questions, demonstrating understanding of the subject under investigation.

CCSS.ELA-Literacy.CCRA.W.10

Write routinely over extended time frames (time for research, reflection, and revision) and shorter time frames (a single sitting or a day or two) for a range of tasks, purposes, and audiences.

CCSS.ELA-Literacy.CCRA.SL.4

Present information, findings, and supporting evidence such that listeners can follow the line of reasoning and the organization, development, and style are appropriate to task, purpose, and audience.

> **CCSS.ELA-Literacy.CCRA.SL.5**
> Make strategic use of digital media and visual displays of data to express information and enhance understanding of presentations.
>
> **CCSS.ELA-Literacy.CCRA.SL.6**
> Adapt speech to a variety of contexts and communicative tasks, demonstrating command of formal English when indicated or appropriate.

To demonstrate their learnings, students will build a website.

Figure 4.11 Website Guidelines

You will be building a website to highlight your learning journey about this Passion Project. You will need to make a page for each section. Here's what you should do:

What to include:

- About the Author
    - Do not include personal information or even your last name
    - Make this about a paragraph or so; it could include lists or bullets.
    - This tells readers about who you are.
- Project Parameters
    - You'll need to summarize what you are doing. You may create a page or you can scan in the worksheet after you've filled it in.
- Book Review
    - You'll need to include a book review of the non-fiction book you read.
    - Use the specific language of book reviews.
- Activity #1 (Give it a name).
- Activity #2 (Give it a name).
- Activity #3 (Give it a name).

Tips

- Don't use too much text. If you must write a large amount, make sure you are paragraphing.
- You can block each paragraph (no indent, two returns after end of section).

- Or, you can indent each paragraph (no spaces, one return after end of section).
- Pay attention to design features—there's lots to do to look cool, but make sure you are able to decipher what is happening.
- Spelling is crucial. Make sure it is all right, then check homonyms (there, their, they're).
- Have fun, but use legible fonts.
- Create fun learning experiences. You don't get a chance to chase your own thoughts too often, so take advantage!
- Use lots of pictures and color.
- Videos are great to add to a website.
- Blog.
- Or, vlog.

This is a new requirement, but given the ease with which I built my own website, I realized that this is a valuable skill to hone. Students will follow a few requirements, but as is the norm with most of the project, they are on their own to follow their creative leanings. The idea for the website came from a conversation I had with one of my students who was planning on applying to a private high school, and he and I talked about how cool it would be to send a link to a website with his application. He could build a website fairly easily, but most importantly, he could showcase himself in a unique and novel way. We talked about having a drop-down menu of academics, athletics, volunteering, scouts, and hobbies. It organized his thinking about what he wanted them to know, and I imagine a school can make a better decision about a student when they have such a visual representation.

The Process Presentation

The culminating assessment is the "Process Presentation" using the website they have created as the tool to guide the audience through their learning experience.

Figure 4.12 Process Presentation Rubric

This is a presentation that **EXPLAINS** the **PROCESS** of your **RESEARCH**, as well as shares some of your **KEY LEARNINGS**. You will be using your website to "walk us through" your project in five to seven minutes. Your website should have tabs, pages, or sections to make navigating this presentation easy. You will need to decide what to include, what to skim over, and what to leave out of your presentation. The goal of this presentation is to **INFORM** your audience of **HOW AND WHAT YOU LEARNED**.

How do you explain process?

- What made you choose this topic?
- What directions did your research take you in? How did this lead to your burning question?
- What were your three learning experiences?
- Which was the most helpful in expanding your knowledge of the topic?
- How have you grown/improved/learned from this experience?

PROCESS PRESENTATION RUBRIC

Learning Target	20–25 points	10–19 points	Under 10 points
I CAN... explain how I learned about the topic. /25	The process is described sequentially and in detail. The audience feels like it is on the journey with you.	The process is described but may not be sequential or appropriately detailed. The audience may feel a little lost because you jump around.	The process is not clear to the audience. It may be out of order or not clear because more details are needed. The audience isn't sure of your journey.
I CAN... use my website as a presentation tool, navigating easily. /25	You are very familiar with your website and how to find what you need to show us what you learned. The website is organized in a way that makes this easy for you and intuitive for the audience.	You are pretty familiar with your website and mostly know how to find what you need to show us what you learned. The website is somewhat difficult to navigate and information isn't where it would seem to make sense.	You don't seem to be familiar with your website and don't seem to know where to look for the information to show us what you learned. The website is disorganized or confusing and could have dead links or mislabeled pages.
I CAN... communicate loudly and clearly, while also making eye contact, and share information without reading. /25	The audience is able to hear you 100% of the time, and understand what you say 100% of the time. You make eye contact frequently and never read from the screen.	The audience is able to hear and understand you most of the time, with only moments that aren't loud and clear. You make eye contact, but you read from the screen occasionally.	The audience is not able to hear you or understand you for significant amounts of time. You don't make adequate eye contact, and you rely on the screen to present.
I CAN... INFORM the audience of my new learnings. /25	The audience learns from your presentation and understands the new information.	The audience is entertained, but new information is lacking or unclear.	The audience is disinterested or inattentive because they are unclear of your goal.
Total: /100	**Comments:**		

This is a short presentation, between five and seven minutes. The projects are so involved and personalized by this point that a student wishing to share everything could speak for my entire class. However, what I ask them to share is their process—essentially their experience of the project. I also want students to hone their presentation skills because by spring they are regulars in the front of the room, and it becomes my mission to fine-tune the skill sets we've been building.

Additionally, for many students, this will be the first presentation they've done alone, without their group. I'm very aware that not everyone they encounter in their further years of schooling will believe in so much collaboration, and I don't want to create a group of needy students who aren't self-sufficient. This presentation is a form of reflection for the students and me, as I see gaps in their understanding and ways I'll need to adjust my instruction the next time around. For example, I recently noted a distinct lack of journal or trade articles in any part of the students' research, many of which would really help my students. I know that next year I'll need to book some time in the library so Mrs. Brew, our Library Media Specialist, will help them learn how to utilize these tools. In this way, their reflections also become mine, and the projects come full circle with another group of students, and as I navigate this cycle of learning for my students, I too learn so much from year to year. Trust me when I tell you that my first attempts at PBL left me with plenty to learn!

Clearly, PBL (any of them, for that matter) is an engaging way to differentiate. Someone asked me, "So, if it's so amazing, why isn't this the model used everywhere?" There are probably many ways to answer that question, but the most straightforward one in my experience is that there are a lot of teachers who are too nervous to try something they perceive as so enormous and amorphous. Some teachers feel that the content would never be "covered," which I've always hated. Don't we want the content to be *learned*? It isn't that we just need to "get through" what the book says or what might be on the test, but instead look at all those different lives in front of you.

I have friends who laugh at me because my plans are two months out; there are others who can't believe I would let students have five workdays; some think I'm nuts to grade students on a collaborative task, or to allow alternate assignments if the students come up with something on their own. Some people think letting parents in my room is the craziest thing I do. Don't get me wrong, I don't do PBL every day; in fact, you've got my two favorite go-to projects here, one for fall and one for spring. But I do differentiate every day, and the BAM I ask for with Project Based

Learning is the guide to what I think students need every day: burning questions, authentic audiences, and teachers who promote Millennial skills. Teachers need to find their own way through this adventure in PBL. It's time to give it a try! Use "Developing PBL for Any Subject!" to get started.

Figure 4.13 Developing PBL for Any Subject!

Use these checklists to develop a project for your classroom

Burning Questions (choose one)	**Authentic Audiences** (unlimited)	**Millennial Skills** (choose three or more)
Social Studies How did technology impact (event)? How could we improve our town? How does ancestry impact us today? How did ancestry impact (group)? Could _____ have been prevented? Will we have another world war? Is there a perfect government? Would anarchy work? ***Science*** Is money driving how we use energy? Can science prevent a natural disaster? How does our waste impact the future? Which invention impacted us the most? What is the next huge invention? ***Health*** Which culture has the healthiest lifestyle? Should we force people to be healthy? Can we prevent pandemics? Is healthcare a right? ***Economics*** Does advertising drive teen spending? Are we responsible for the homeless? What does money have to do with crime? Is there financial freedom? ***Math*** How can we reduce waste? When will the next natural disaster occur? What would be a better infrastructure? How does symmetry impact society? What is the best design for a sports arena?	teachers students parents administrators government the elderly younger kids older kids companies other classes organizations libraries museums galleries publishers artists scientists doctors lawyers designers inventors friends neighborhoods pen pals technicians clergy volunteers fundraisers coaches stores planners each other	utilize technology read research write a summary analyze results identify resources interview experts plan a project apply formulas or codes design and create measure and calculate locate places assemble a product create an outline reflect continually build models or prototypes answer questions organize ideas present findings create presentations collaborate in person collaborate digitally globalize thinking write code read code do a demonstration make a Prezi create with Canva design a Haiku Deck curate an exhibit host a Q and A session participate in a debate judge a debate

Your Turn

Think about your own classroom!

- *All types of PBL are about extended learning experiences.* How long do you think it will take for you to do a project like this?
- *BAM is the key.* What will you do to help students discover their burning question?
- *Embracing the chaos is crucial.* What feelings are you going to have to overcome in order to let organic learning happen?
- *It all takes longer than you think.* What dates, activities, assemblies, and vacations do you need to consider as you plan?
- *Intentionally establish the behaviors you want to see.* What is most important to you—noise level, location of students, on-task working, or something else?
- *Allow organic mini-lessons to develop.* Are there some go-to topics that you know your students always need to review?
- *Technology is a Millennial must.* How can you prepare and provide the technology for learning?
- *Presentations ensure students will remember forever.* Can you make your students' presentations special by inviting parents, administrators, or other students?

5

Assessment

Valuing the Individual in a Standardized World

I'm not going to talk much about standardized testing except to say that in my career it has been a necessary evil, as it is likely a part of yours as well. I have to write and administer Student Learning Objectives (SLOs); my Annual Professional Performance Review (APPR) is weighted to include performance of my students on controversial state assessments; and I have tried to involve myself with the testing process as much as possible. Wait, you might be thinking: Why would someone who is such a big proponent of differentiation want to work on *standardized* tests? The answer is simple. Whenever educational decisions are being made, I want a seat at the table. I never pretend to agree when I don't, and I feel better knowing what my students are up against.

My devotion to differentiation does not mean I've abandoned traditional test taking, as I would not want to do my students the disservice of never teaching how to be assessed using the dominant methodology. No matter how archaic I find some parts of standardized testing to be, I feel strongly that I need to prepare my students for their path ahead, and until colleges start accepting portfolios and personal websites instead of SAT and AP scores, I'll teach the basic psychology behind multiple choice tests and the formula for effective test writing.

Assessment ◆ 111

Figure 5.1 Multiple Choice Strategies (Secrets to Standardized Success!)

Multiple choice tests are designed to check your understanding of a passage you read, determine if you are making the correct inferences, and check your vocabulary skills. The tests are designed around a concept of "best answer" and "distractor" as the top two answers, and two other answers that are either completely wrong or will appeal to a misunderstanding that you might have.

For example: What is the meaning of the word "hoarse" in this sentence?

The young boy was hoarse after a long day working and yelling in the fields.

A) strong and powerful [*attributes of a horse*]
B) raspy and harsh [*the actual definition*]
C) tired and silent [*an inference you could make, incorrectly*]
D) quiet and tired [*second best answer; distractor that is close, but not best/most accurate*]

Letter A is simply meant to be an answer that is *associated with a misconception* about the word horse instead of hoarse. It is meant to trip up careless readers.
Letter B is the answer.
Letter C is *an assumption* that you would be tired and not want to talk after your day.
Letter D *is close*, as raspy is quiet, and tired is how your voice becomes raspy.
SO . . . What can you do to avoid the trickery?! Use this TIP!

T—trust your first thought

Don't read the answers! Before you even look at the answers, think of the answer. Then, you are looking for that answer instead of starting with nothing and being persuaded of the wrong answer. Match what you thought of with the correct choice.

I—identify the distractor

Find the two answers that match what you were thinking. Identify the distractor by determining if it is too strong (all, always, never), grammatically incorrect (wrong tense, verb instead of noun), or is close to a wrong answer.

P—play the game

The test makers are trying to determine if you are a *good* AND *careful* reader. Read all the answers because frequently the distractor comes first, and if you are impulsive and *NOT a careful reader*, you'll be tricked into picking the wrong answer. Remember that you can look back at the text, even if it doesn't ask you to—because *careful* readers know that.

Figure 5.2 Test Writing

CL (claim):

> You must make a claim about the prompt that is provided. It is not just restating, but has the answer in the sentence.

E (example):

> You need to use a transition to introduce this (for example, additionally, also, clearly, in this way, on the other hand, therefore, consequently, subsequently, thus, finally, however). This will be a short quote from the text or a few important words.

e (explain the example):

> *This means that* . . . or *The author shows us here* . . . or *The text indicates* . . . or *The purpose of these words* . . . or *The reader can tell that* . . . or *One may infer that* . . .

E (example):

> This is a DIFFERENT example or detail from the text. It will also be quoted words from the text. Must use a different transition word to introduce the example.

e (explain the example):

> Explain the text, just as you did in the first example.

R (restate your claim):

> Use strong language (clearly, obviously, as evidenced here, this proves that, demonstrated here).

Prompt: Cinderella undergoes transformation in the story. Explain how the author creates this effect.

> **CL**: Cinderella undergoes both physical and psychological transformations over the course of the story.
> **E**: *For example*, the Fairy Godmother and animals help her transform from a "lowly peasant" to a beautiful potential "princess" by giving her a makeover on the outside.
> **e**: This is important because the action of the story depends on her being at the ball, which she could not do in her original state.
> **E**: *Additionally*, the author orchestrates a psychological transformation as Cinderella gains confidence and understands her true worth.
> **e**: This is accomplished through the Prince's desire to find her, as well as the change in her demeanor when out of her evil stepmother's home.
> **R**: *Clearly*, the physical and psychological transformations are at the heart of the author's purpose in telling this story.

This is a modification of the popular CEE paragraph. (Claim, Evidence, Evidence).

Though test writing and prep is covered, most of this chapter will help you sort through your own notions of why we grade, what fair means, and how assessing learning is different from grading it.

> ### Sneak Peek
>
> In this chapter, you'll explore . . .
>
> - *multiple choice and short answer standardized test strategies*
> - *what it means to "show what you know"*
> - *why "everything counts"*
> - *how to encourage your students that they must "be your best self"*
> - *paradoxical questions*
> - *why "fair" isn't really the question*
> - *the difference between grading and assessment.*

The Future Is EQ, Not IQ

However, for the most part, instead of focusing on standardized testing, I take a balanced approach to teaching reading, writing, speaking, listening, and the soft skills that are crucial for our students. The future is going to be more about EQ (Emotional Quotient) than it is about IQ (Intelligence Quotient). The characteristics that were the mark of success in the last century—memory, computation, and raw knowledge—will be trumped by innovation, collaboration, and relationships. If I were to break my philosophy into those inspirational posters you see in a doctor's office, they would be: SHOW WHAT YOU KNOW, EVERYTHING COUNTS, and BE YOUR BEST SELF. That educational agenda on my part might not seem demanding; however, I think that you'll see replacing cookie cutter compliance with engaged risk taking is far more rigorous than many people believe, and importantly, far more relevant.

Show What You Know

At the heart of differentiation is a sincere appreciation of students' talents, personalities, fears, and past failures. There is no way a teacher with as many students as I have can know the individual learning story that each child brings in carefully organized, overflowing backpacks each year. However, I make it a point to find out as much as I can, so that I can create learning experiences that let them "show what you know." There's more about this information gathering process in Chapter 6 on Family Partnerships.

Because students are all unique, I believe that a unit should not be assessed by a single measure. For example, after reading *The Giver*, we had an objective test to mirror standardized test requirements, and a project and presentation that each counted as a test grade. This way, if students struggle with a particular type of assessment, s/he is able to "show what s/he knows" in a way that traditional tests can't. I have an interesting situation this year in that I have twins on my team of students, each very different. The mother sent me this email, and it reinforced what I am trying to do:

> This is Lori Zak, Kyle and Luke's mom. I just wanted to say THANK YOU for all the hard work that you are doing with my guys in ELA. I don't think that they have ever been quite as challenged as they have been this year, and you have definitely made them step up to that challenge. The projects and assignments that you are giving them are so meaningful and worthwhile (LOVE the Fishbowl activity) that you are making them want to do well and be better students. Lucas has always had a love for ELA, but this year, so far, has really brought out the best in him. Kyle has always struggled in ELA (Math is his area of strength). He is also not a great test taker. Never has been. This year, however, you have given Kyle the opportunity to improve his grades with all of the other activities that you are giving him to do. You have restored a great deal of the confidence that Kyle has lost over the years. For that, I am sincerely grateful.

But It Feels Like I'm Breaking the Rules . . .

The reason I share that email is that, if you choose to embrace differentiation in all aspects of your teaching, you will feel—or at least I do—that I am breaking some rule of how my classroom is supposed to run. There are times when things feel sloppy and messy, and students are struggling, and I am trying to let them, but I just want to swoop in and tell them how to do it. But, that is not the point of differentiation. If I give them space, and I facilitate instead of dominate, students are capable of some pretty amazing things, and they find ways to impress me all the time. Additionally, if I am able to find ways for students to show what they know, I put the responsibility squarely on their shoulders, and for some, help them reestablish a confidence and love of learning that years of traditional testing have eroded.

Connect Content to Meaningful Learning

The one tenet of differentiation that changed every aspect of my class is this: You can assess students on what they know, in any way that demonstrates the knowledge that was gained. This means that unless you are assessing multiple choice test-taking skills, your students do not have to take a multiple choice test. When the format of the assessment is not the centerpiece of the conversation, learning is deeper, richer, and allows students an opportunity to show what *they* know instead of show how well they can guess what *you* wanted them to know.

Again, I don't abandon teaching students what I know they need to know, but the key element of successful unit planning is managing the standards that you wish to assess and offering a variety of activities to meet the needs of all types of students. I've sat down with colleagues and talked about a unit, and we'd end up sitting there shaking our heads trying to create an assessment on half the Common Core! This part is hard. This part is, for me, radical. *I don't have to assess everything, every time.* I have begun limiting myself to five "power standards" to address during a unit. I do two units per quarter, so this means I'll explore (not "cover" or "hit") forty standards in the course of a year. Once I realized how much more my students retained when the content is connected to meaningful learning experiences, I knew this was the way for me to incorporate standards into a differentiated classroom.

Allowing learning to dictate assessment is not easy to implement, and in my case, it was downright nerve wracking. I'm a neurotic planner, a devotee of Wiggins and McTighe's *Understanding by Design*, and a reformed (almost) grade hound myself. The good news is that for those like me who need checklists and organization, the best way to plan a project is with the end in mind. This would translate across most subject areas, limited mostly by the specific demands of content the curriculum requires; obviously, the Humanities are easier to differentiate over, say, Math. Math and Science standards and requirements, for the most part, require a stricter adherence to a scope and sequence mapped by the teacher or textbook because some skills are prerequisites for those that come next. For those subject areas that are the most rigid in terms of chronology and content, I'd suggest leveling the playing field a bit by offering as many choices as possible.

Everything Counts

There is nothing I hate more than sloppy work. I've always wanted students to hand in their best work, of course. However, when technology is readily available, a page ripped from a notebook and written in hieroglyphics is just not going to cut it. If you are required to handwrite on a test or in class activity, you should spend nearly as much time making it look nice as you do thinking of the answer. No one wants to admit this, but everyone makes an assessment of quality based on presentation. Good teachers obviously move past the chocolate milk on the paper or all capital letters because the girl who dots her i's with hearts says, "I just write like that." Unfortunately, the rest of the world is going to take one look at some of the "junk" that teachers accept and never give it another glance. This may sound harsh, but I think one of the greatest disservices we can do to young people right now is to ignore the obvious: We are really being assessed all the time. It is happening every day, everywhere, about every aspect of how we present ourselves and our work.

I ask my students, "What do you think it says about your work if you didn't put your name on it? It looks like you don't care very much about the work that you do, which makes me think I probably shouldn't hire you, or give you an internship, or accept your application, because if you don't take care of the little things like this, you'll never be able to handle the big stuff. *You have to know that yes, everything counts.* Always. That means handwriting. That means spelling. That means neatness. That means complete sentences. That means looking people in the eye. That means speaking loudly and clearly. Above all, it means everything matters, everywhere—not just in ELA." This comes across as sounding like a neurotic ELA teacher crossed with an inspirational speaker, but if that's what it takes to get them to listen, I'm all for it.

All Teachers Need to Hold Students Accountable

Teachers also must realize that we are preparing students for these "life assessments" that happen all the time. Whose job is this? Are you thinking, wait, I teach Science? Or, I'm a Physical Education teacher. How is this my job? It is every teacher's job. *All* subjects. Our job, collectively, is to prepare students for the real world. I'm not suggesting we grade students on their handwriting or the margins on their papers, but it is crucial that we do hold students accountable for the expectations that technology has dictated. Spelling mistakes? Unacceptable. Coming to class and saying "I didn't remember what a metaphor was" as an excuse is over. I regularly ask my students, "What do you do if you don't understand a task? Look. It. Up. Find an example. Google 'metaphors for kids' and study it." With the world literally and physically at the end of their fingertips, we must train students to use their resources because information is NOT the commodity of this century. It's the given. What students do with that information is what is going to be important in their future, and unless we are clear to them that the information is the prerequisite, they are going to fall behind.

Harness the Interest in Social Media and Technology

According to the article by the Pew Research Center, "Teens, Social Media and Technology Overview 2015," "Aided by the convenience and constant access provided by mobile devices, especially smartphones, 92% of teens report going online daily—including 24% who say they go on 'almost constantly'" (Lenhart, 2015, p. 1). We must harness this attraction, while also teaching digital literacy because EVERYTHING COUNTS. The decision making tools students have are not fully developed, and they must be told over and over, in as many ways as possible, that their digital footprint is permanent and in their future, EVERYTHING COUNTS. Colleges and universities don't like to admit that they "spy" on potential students; however, there are many surveys that say between 50% and 70% of colleges google students and/or look at social media activity. My plan to help my students? We are creating websites of their Passion Projects, as described earlier in the Project Based Learning chapter.

This is new to me, and I'll be trying it out soon, but my goal is to meet them where they are, and in this case, it is online. Creating a website is not overly difficult because we are using Wix, a free website. However, helping students understand the power of their footprint is challenging, but I am excited to show them that if what they put online is worthwhile, that is what they are "putting out there" to the world. After we've built the websites, I'm going to have students google their names, and they'll find the website, and I'll teach them about SEO (search engine optimization). They are going to be super-proud of what these projects and their websites say about them as students—the sites will be creative, innovative, and involve a passion of theirs; they will also be polished, due to a dedicated group of editors in our class.

This second part of my philosophy regarding assessment goes hand in hand with "show what you know." Students will be demonstrating their competencies, showcasing their talents, and learning the importance of their online identity. I'm going to encourage them to keep their websites active, and I will show them the blogging features and suggest ways to help them build to it. Imagine you are that college admissions officer who is "not really" spying but googles a student's name, and instead of the typical selfies and self-indulgent posts she finds a webpage. The webpage shows the admissions officer several things: an authentic writing sample, presumed technological prowess, the "stick-to-itiveness" of maintaining a website, and a digital collage of the student's passions and interests. No matter what an admissions officer says, this will turn out far more impressive than yet another "person I most admire" essay.

Perhaps this isn't what comes to mind when you hear the word *assessment*, but ask anyone who has tried to find a job in the last five years what mattered most in their job search. Most of the time, it is a *relationship* that gets a person in the door. Now, once you are there, you have to prove you are the best candidate, but when there are 300 people applying for the same job, an "in" is important. That "in" can be created by setting yourself apart from the crowd by the person you put out into the world via the Internet and taking advantage of the fact that "everything counts."

Helping Students Be Their Best Selves

There's an interesting conversation going on right now in the world of assessment, something I find more important to my particular teaching situation than the continual buzz about standardization. Mark Barnes, author of *Assessment 3.0* and publisher of the *Hack Learning* Series, well-known educator, speaker, and no-grades advocate, has stirred the pot a bit. He suggests that grades are not a true measure of learning, and in fact are detrimental to students' reaching their full potential. I'm most interested in the conversations that are growing from his perpetual questioning of why we grade the way we do. The chances of my not assigning grades are minuscule; much like most schools, we have prescribed ways of grading. However, another question bubbled to the surface through Twitter chats, Facebook posts, and blog posts: Does a student have to perform above and *beyond* the standards to receive an "A," or is an "A" the mark of mastery?

Paradoxical Questions

If you think I have the answer to that paradoxical question, I appreciate your faith in me; nevertheless, I don't have the answer, but I have more questions to add:

- Is a Special Education student, who is receiving modifications to the assignment, entitled to the same "A" as other students?
- Should my ENL (English as a New Language) student complete the same work to earn the same grade as other students, even if she doesn't read English well?
- If a student meets every requirement on a rubric at the highest level, is that a 100%, or am I expecting him/her to complete some amorphous requirement to get that perfect 100%?
- If I have five teachers grade the same paper, using the same rubric, and we end up with a twenty-four-point difference, is there any evidence that grading is objective? (This really happened!)
- If a student receives a 100% on a pretest, why does he have to complete the unit?
- If a student hands in work late, yet it is fabulous or even brilliant, should she lose a letter grade?

If I were to guess, I'd venture to say that the biggest difference in opinion among teachers is grading, which of course makes sense, since I believe assessing students is one of the trickiest aspects of teaching, and one that we come under fire for often. There are many examples of ways to assess students in this book, yet when I've taught classes about differentiation, the one area that still stumps teachers is grading. The word "fair" comes up, over and over, and honestly I was hung up on it for a while, too.

Grading and Assessing Are Not the Same Thing

However, if we have the best interests of the students in mind, it is clear to me that "grading" and "assessing" are actually at odds with each other. Grading is assigning a rank to the quality of work a child does. Assessing is gauging, evaluating, and weighing a student's understanding, ostensibly in order to provide correction and advice on how to improve. How often, though, do teachers assign the grade, wait to hand back the quizzes until everyone has made it up, and upon returning it see that students no longer care? They've moved on, and it is no longer relevant to their lives or learning.

Above All: Feedback

To combat this, I'm far more concerned with feedback than I am with anything else. I'll admit, I don't have this mastered, but every time I assess students, I try to make the grading turn around as quick as possible and provide comments. This year for my annual observation, my principal, Ryan Sikorski, was there to witness the Fishbowl activity in this book. The students knew what they were doing, the moderator kept the questions moving, and I was scribbling—as fast as I could—notes to each person on their individual rubrics. I interjected when necessary, but I was definitely *a* facilitator, not even *the* facilitator, as the volunteer student moderator was really far more "in control" than I was of the situation. In my pre-conference with Ryan, I explained what he would see, and I expressed my concern that he might not be comfortable with observing me in this role since I wouldn't be "teaching" in a way that seemed traditional. However, I walked through the rubric with him and noted that to receive the highest rating on the Charlotte Danielson rubric we use, students must be in charge of their own learning, self-correct, self-monitor, and achieve synchronicity with their class members' needs. Ryan is a forward-thinking guy, so he didn't see a problem with it, and recognized that students don't magically know how to run a Fishbowl, self-regulate, or know how to converse with one another academically. He also knows that I am constantly adding another layer to their individual performance expectations. The fact is, the highest level of academic achievement for our students comes when they are pushing themselves to levels they have not achieved before, not stopping at the prescribed level that equals an "A," or worse, not being able to reach that level and therefore not even attempting to be the best they can be.

Always Value the Student Over the Grading

We must instill in our students the love of learning and exploring, an attitude that almost all children have until they come to school, where the natural curiosity they'd enjoyed before is relocated to a grade. We so often act as if tangential questions are a distraction, not the actual point of the lesson—to make students dig deeper, make connections, and internalize learning. When students know they are more than a grade—because you tell them so by the time, effort, and quality of the feedback you give them—they are willing to work hard for you, but more importantly, for themselves. This isn't easy. There are definitely more questions than answers here. That doesn't mean you shouldn't try to create the best classroom for your students.

Your Turn

Want to start your own feedback loop? Are you ready to assess instead of grade? Here's what you'll need to remember:

- *Standardized tests are probably here to stay.* How can you incorporate testing strategies into your daily routines so that there's not "test prep" per se?
- *Show what you know.* Which ways will you accept for students to demonstrate learning: visually, audibly, artistically, theatrically?
- *Everything counts.* How can you ensure your students know this?
- *Be your best self.* Consider how this idea has evolved with technology.

- *We must all ponder our own paradoxical questions.* What troubles you about this chapter? This book?
- *Is that fair?* Is this a relevant question?
- *There is a difference between grading and assessing.* Can you change the paradigm in your classroom?

6

Family Partnerships

Creating a Customized "Dream Team" for Students

I'm not proud of it, but family and school partnerships weren't my major priority until I had children of my own; to be honest, there was no way I could comprehend what it felt like to send my little people off to school. The first time I realized that I wouldn't know what they were doing once they walked through the elaborately decorated kindergarten door, I almost had a nervous breakdown. Would the teacher be nice? What if my child wasn't learning? What if my child got in trouble? Do the people in that building care about my kiddo? What if she is having a bad day? What if my son drifts off into his own little world? There were so many things I wanted to tell the teacher! How do parents do this, I wondered. From that day forward, my practice changed dramatically. I knew that before I could enlist the help of parents in best educating their children, I needed to let them know who I was and give them the opportunity to tell me about their child.

Sneak Peek

In this chapter, you will . . .

- *learn how to close the gap between school and family*
- *develop relationships with families that celebrate the student*
- *deepen understanding of your students*
- *use the family as a valuable expert on the student*
- *conduct a productive family and school conference.*

How Will Families Perceive You and Your Classroom?

I had to overcome the self-conscious feeling that I was babbling on about myself and about my classroom, and that I was adding insult to injury by meddling in their family life. I created a "Welcome to ELA" sheet that seems much like any other welcome to school letter.

Figure 6.1 Welcome to ELA Sheet

Welcome to a New Year!

Hello and welcome back. There will be lots of information coming home over the next few days, so I will keep this simple. This will be an exciting year for your child, and I am here to help guide him/her through all the new experiences. I am a National Board Certified teacher, and it is my pleasure to work with YOU and your child to make this a great year. The curriculum is challenging, but I am confident in our ability to work together. I am a mom of two, Zoey (10) and Oliver (7), so I can truly appreciate that school is a child's "home away from home." I also do not assign homework due the next day, as I appreciate the many extras that we all have in our lives and the need to spend time together. *If you ever need anything—even if it is for me to let you know what kind of day your child is having or if he remembered his instrument—please don't hesitate to email me, and I will get back to you ASAP.*

Your child is going to need a one-inch binder, any color, with five sections/dividers. I'm going to do my best to help the less-than-organized stay on top of things. I myself am an organizational and planning geek, so I'll give the kiddos lots of ways to strategize against the gigantic pile of school stuff that accumulates. Students will be able to access what they need from my website, AmberRainChandler.com, so the paper load will not be as heavy. Please subscribe to the website, and you'll get the updates automatically. Students also need a few packages of lined paper—which they can keep or give to me—I'll always make sure they have some. Also, you child will need pens or pencils.

Please provide the following information if you'd like to be on my email blast. I send copies of the PowerPoints, assignments, and reminders. I encourage students and parents to sign up.

Your name: _____
Your email: _____
Your child's name: _____
Your child's email: _____
Your phone number (if you want texts, videos, or photos sent to you): _____

Philosophies and Expectations

- ◆ Projects are the best way to learn.
- ◆ There are basic expectations for ALL students to be successful. Writing complete sentences and using appropriate capitalization and punctuation will be required at all times. If your child needs help, I will run review sessions after school and provide extra practice to bring him/her up to speed.
- ◆ I will not assign "next day" homework. I want to respect your family time and child's other interests; however, there will almost always be a project going on, and students should read. Managing time is a very big lesson of 8th grade.
- ◆ Confident speakers have an edge over everyone else.
- ◆ Everything is a rough draft. I'm about the learning, not the grade. If your child isn't getting something, I will help him/her to keep working on it until they have the skill down and the grade they want. There are a few exceptions to this, and I will let you and your child know when something is "final." The opportunity to improve the grade comes with significant remediation. Your child won't be just taking something over and over, or correcting mistakes. Your child will actually learn what they need to learn!
- ◆ Everything matters. I will teach students why handing in quality work ALWAYS matters, why class participation is crucial, and why they should put their "best self" out there for the world to see.
- ◆ I embrace technology. Type it. Email it. Share it with me. Your child will be allowed, on occasion, to use his/her device in class. Technology forms will follow.
- ◆ It is crucial that my classroom is a safe and welcoming place, setting the vibe for success. You will be notified to meet with your child and our team if there is ever an indication of bullying.
- ◆ I'm one of "those people" who checks email often, so that's the best way to get to me. Leave your number if you'd like me to call you.
- ◆ Students may bring a snack and water to drink. No peanuts. Hydration and nutrition is crucial for growing kids (and hungry adults).

Every child needs at least one involved, committed adult at school. I hope I am that person for your child!

In my version, I added a "My Philosophies and Expectations" list on the back, telling myself that parents could take it or leave it. I encourage you to think about your classroom through the eyes of a parent who might not have liked school or maybe did not do very well. Classrooms are intimidating, and I've been in one every year since I was five, either as a student or teacher! Before you send out your mini-manifesto, brainstorm your feelings and thoughts about these topics:

- Homework
- Family vacations
- Retakes or do-overs
- Discipline
- Responsibility
- Eating or drinking in the classroom
- Respect/bullying/adult interventions into kids' lives
- The ways you think students learn best.

Once you've come up with a list of school topics, you might also consider if you want to share personal information. I have found that sharing a little about myself is a good icebreaker. I usually just talk about my kids, but depending on where you live, sharing sports-related information ("die-hard Bills fan" or "I live for hockey games") can go a long way in bridging the gap between home and school. The chasm between teacher and parents is usually crossed by stretching poor students across the divide, so finding a way to reach out immediately is important. In my experience, if I address parents as the experts on their child, they will better trust me to be the expert in the classroom.

Let Parents Know You *Really* See *Their* Child

The beginning of the year is so hectic that this suggestion is going to sound crazy: Call or email every parent before you have to handle a single student issue. Rik Rowe, a high school math teacher, and Anabel Gonzalez, an ESL teacher, founded a Twitter chat called #GCHchat (GoodCallsHome) that encourages teachers to make those connections home ASAP and to keep those calls going throughout the school year to foster family participation and improve student achievement. I admire the idea of making all those calls—and I admit that it is probably more effective than what I do, but I believe that all of us, as teachers, have to find what will actually work for us. Hearing from a teacher in a positive way—no matter the method—is an awesome experience.

For the first few weeks of school, I send between five and ten emails a day until every parent has been contacted. It doesn't have to be lengthy, and mine aren't. I try to zero in on something specific I notice about their child. I want parents to know that I am paying attention, that I am actually *seeing* their child, not as one in a sea of many faces, but as an individual. The style of the email should meet your communication style. Here are a few that I sent this year:

> *Just a quick note to let you know that your son has amazing manners. When I was passing out papers today, he was the first to say "Thank You," and that started a chain reaction. I'm looking forward to more of his positive leadership this year. Please pass on a "great job" from me!*

> *I wanted to touch base with you and let you know what a great day your daughter had in class today. We were reviewing some of our Greek roots, and she was on fire! I can tell she's been studying, and I commend her dedication to school work. Pass on to her that I want her to keep up the class participation. She's making my job easier!*

> *Wow! is all I can say about the amazing show of kindness I noticed today. Your son was leaving the classroom when another student dropped his stuff, and the contents of his pencil case went flying. Your son turned around, came back into the room, and helped the student. As they were leaving, I said, "That was so nice to help your friend like that," and your son told me he didn't even know who it was! This is good stuff. Please let your son know I am impressed.*

Here's the best part: Writing these emails changes my perspective on students. I look for the best in these new faces, and it never ceases to amaze me what great stuff is happening right in front of me that I wouldn't notice unless I was looking for it. I continue sending emails sporadically throughout the year, but if I write a negative email, I then write five positive ones before I leave the computer as a reminder of the positives all around me and the obligation I have to those students to *see* them too.

Acknowledge Families as Experts on Their Children

I give parents the first week to be inundated with all the other things to sign before I send home the "Family Share Sheet."

Figure 6.2 Family Share Sheet

CONFIDENTIAL: Please send me your answers via email or return in an envelope!

What is your child really good at? Could be computers, volleyball, running, gaming, making movies—whatever. Everyone is really good at something, so help me to understand how to motivate your child.
_____
_____

What is hard for your child to do? Is there a "history" to something that I need to know? This can be academic, social, emotional, or a combination.
_____
_____

Tell me about your child's *reading and writing habits*.
_____
_____

Is there something I should know about you that might be helpful for me to understand your child? This is where you can share family history (death of a sibling, divorce, etc.), your child's health, or school history. Also, if your child is very sensitive about a topic, let me know.
_____
_____

Does your child have other adults in the building who s/he cares about? I try to build a group of "cheerleaders" in the building to share in the successes of your child.
_____
_____

Do you have any topic, job, writing, or hobby that I can beg you to come *talk to us* about?
_____
_____

If there is someone you *would not want your child sitting near*, let me know:
_____
_____

Is there anyone *who you know who is "good for"* your child to work with:
_____
_____

Anything else?
_____
_____

⬬

As they come back in, I read them, noting anything that requires immediate attention, and I start an individual file on each student, stapling this sheet to the inside of the folder. I take a few minutes to review each sheet, noting any trends I see across my students. For example, I've had years with a large number of artists, and other times, I've had students who love creative writing. If I can plan lessons that teach to their interests, I have a better chance of catching their attention. Additionally, before I make a call, send an email, or have a meeting with a parent, I refresh myself about the family and the perceptions the parent has about their child. For example, if I have a mom who is worried about her son's lack of friendships, I can offer insights about that as a part of the conversation.

The companion to the "Family Share Sheet" is the "Top Secret Stuff" student information sheet.

⬬

Figure 6.3 Top Secret Stuff

Confidential (Pinky Promise!)

What are you really good at? Could be computers, volleyball, running, gaming, making movies . . . whatever. Everyone is really good at something. Hidden talents? Hobbies? Interests? Don't be shy. I won't share with anyone!
_____
_____

What is hard for you to do? Could be make friends, swim, eat broccoli, read, dance, public speaking . . . you get the idea!
_____
_____

Tell me about something you read over the summer (Internet, magazines, directions, books, emails, texts, whatever).
_____
_____

Is there something I should know about you that might be helpful for me to know? In the past, students have told me that they split living between two places, they have a deceased sibling or family member, they have a disease or illness, etc. It could be simply that you love (or hate) ELA!
_____
_____

What do you think the most important part of school is for you? Friends? Sports? Learning (OMG!)? Being in drama club or on student council . . . you get the idea.
_____
_____

Name two students you might like to sit near:
_____
_____

Is there anyone you would rather not work with for personal reasons?
_____
_____

Favorite song: _____ Favorite movie: _____

I usually give this sheet to students within the first few weeks of school, usually in some downtime that happens as a result of assemblies or shortened schedules. I have students complete these in class, but I always tell them to email me anything that they didn't think of at the time. This sheet, combined with the "Family Share Sheet," can offer important insights into the family and help me to understand how to differentiate my communication or level of support for the student. For example, if both the child and parent mention the student's anxiety about tests, I might send an email before the first test with some "tips," which I will likely already have covered in class. This gesture can put everyone at ease and set the tone. Sometimes the information is devastatingly hard to bear—a deceased parent, a crippling medical condition, or painful shyness, but it is cases like this that make the communication all the more important.

Forming a Partnership

Larry Ferlazzo, a high school English teacher and author of *Building Parent Engagement in Schools* (with Lorie Hammond) (Linworth, 2009) and *Helping Students Motivate Themselves: Practical Answers to Classroom Problems* (Routledge, 2011), has been examining how families impact student learning for a long time. In "Involvement or Engagement?" in the May 2011 *Educational Leadership*, Ferlazzo explains,

> A school striving for family involvement often leads with its mouth—identifying projects, needs, and goals and then telling parents how they can contribute. A school striving for parent engagement, on the other hand, tends to lead with its ears—listening to what parents think, dream, and worry about. The goal of family engagement is not to serve clients but to gain partners.
>
> (p. 1)

In the classroom, this is the equivalent of asking parents to send in treats for a party versus asking them what kind of party they might want to have.

Too often we become so engrossed in our curriculum, projects, or simple day-to-day tasks that we forget why we are there in the first place, and we need that gentle reminder: We teach children. Forming partnerships is great when the sailing is smooth, but it is even more important when the waters are choppy.

Five Tips for an Effective Conference With Parents

1. Set Parameters
Full disclosure here. I once spent 35 minutes at a parent conference for one of my children that was supposed to be 15 minutes long. I more than doubled the time allotted to me. So, when parents want to go on and on, they are not likely devaluing your time, but just getting on a roll like I did and losing track of the time.

If you are meeting alone with a parent (which I don't recommend in most situations), then you'll need to let the parent know up front that you have a specific amount of time. If you are meeting with a team, the person least involved should mention the time parameter. Any meeting over a half hour, unless for very serious situations, is likely too long.

Time saver: Rehashing situations can be perceived as piling on, particularly if there is more than one teacher in the meeting. There is nothing wrong with saying, "I'm seeing the same thing with Suzy that Mr. Smith described."

2. The Parents Are the Experts About Their Child

As I mentioned, it goes a long way to defer to a parent about his or her child. Sometimes they aren't the expert, but it's a wise attitude to assume. If you enter a meeting with a superior attitude about your deep understanding of this person's baby (and they are, no matter the age, all babies in their parent's eyes), then the parent is immediately on the defensive. Instead, ask questions. For example, "Billy has an inconsistent homework grade. Is there anything you can tell me to help me understand what is going on in that area?" You may full well know that the parent is not supportive or that this child plays video games all night, but it is better to let him or her come to that realization than for you to make accusations. I mention this piece of advice because I think that a parent who is playing defense is likely the cause of most misunderstandings.

I am a teacher, fully versed in theoretical approaches to parent communication and collaboration, and yet I have walked into a meeting in my parent role anxious and frustrated, feeling like my good name is somehow on the line. My shoulders are tensed up and my mental motor is roaring along with a combination of excuses and insinuations. Now imagine the parent who hasn't been inside a school in twenty years, approaching the teacher's desk like a child sent to the principal's office. Incidentally, don't sit behind your desk. I wouldn't even suggest your classroom. If possible, find a neutral space in a conference room, library, or office.

3. Don't Come Empty-Handed

Parents have very little idea what exemplary work should look like, or what their child is actually doing at school. In many cases, class expectations are unclear at best and certainly nothing like their own experience.

Bring samples of their child's work—both the good and the not so good. Show the parents examples of what grade-level work would look like, obviously removing the names. Give the parent a printed out, in-progress, grade report. Show how a student's grade can be significantly better if the student's quiz average improved, even doing the math right in front of them. Help them to understand that all is not lost and improvement is possible. If, by the way, the student cannot recover, the meeting was definitely too late and all sides should own that.

We've all heard, time after time, that data should inform our instruction. Parents are not operating from that place. They love their child, don't know what to do, and don't have accurate information about their child's performance. On the same note, don't mislead a parent into believing that their child is an "A" student hiding in a "D" body, unless that is true.

Sometimes, no matter how hard the child tries or what turnaround plan is developed, the child is not going to reach the highest level of proficiency. The focus should be on making significant progress, and the child should certainly be lauded for major improvement. The goal of parent–teacher relationships should be optimizing the experience of the student and measuring learning, not points.

4. Have a Plan, But Ask for the Parent's Plan First

Generally, a parent has not taken time off from work to just discuss a problem. Instead, parents are looking for concrete steps that are going to be taken to solve their problem. Very likely, you have a pretty good idea of what would help, but again, defer to the parent first. Almost always the solution is really simple, as in "someone at home needs to make sure he's doing his homework." But it's better for the parent to be empowered than for you to seem like you are scolding them. Collaboration is always going to trump going it alone, and a student's success is very often the result of a whole team of adults.

If the parents don't seem able to put together a plan, then "How about this? What if Tommy had to show you the completed homework, even if he says he finished it in study hall? That way, you'll be assured that it is actually complete. If we are still having problems after a few weeks, we can strategize again." This "School and Family Team Meeting" form is helpful in establishing what happened at the meeting, as well as the expectations for change.

Figure 6.4 School and Family Team Meeting Form

Please sign below to indicate you were here and strategizing to help!

Student:	Family Member(s):
Teachers:	Administrator(s):
Guidance Counselor:	Other:

Strengths:

___ respectful and polite
___ cooperative
___ socially appropriate
___ great attendance
___ seeks help/good self-advocate
___ on time to class
___ focused/uses time wisely
___ creative
___ problem solver
___ helps other students
___ good test taker
___ completes homework carefully

Areas to grow:

___ disrespectful or rude without thinking
___ uncooperative
___ sometimes not socially appropriate
___ absent often
___ does not express needs
___ late to class
___ distracted/wastes time in class
___ won't take risks expressing self
___ gives up too easily
___ distracts other students
___ struggles with tests
___ does not complete homework or sloppy

Possible solutions for student:

___ eight hours of sleep ___ write down all assignments ___ stay after school ___ eat breakfast
___ tutor or "study buddy" ___ move seat ___ clean out locker and/or backpack
___ participate in class ___ go to website, Quizlet, or other online review ___ complete homework
___ re-route locker trips to be on time ___ do a "check out" with the teacher

Possible solutions for family:

> ___ monitor screen time (use as incentive?) ___ establish scheduled bedtime ___ set up homework/study area ___ check online grades weekly ___ sign homework ___ establish clear consequences ___ do review activities online with your child ___ email teachers to check in ___ check the school website for activities

Possible solutions for teachers:

> ___ sign agenda ___ move seat ___ stay after school ___ print a progress report ___ provide copy of notes ___ offer additional practice assignments ___ find a student helper ___ check in during study hall ___ redirect more often ___ give student a sign to be on task

Other ideas:

This way, if a second meeting is required, the game plan is a helpful reference tool. After the meeting is over, make copies of the completed form for everyone who attended the meeting—including the child.

5. Thank Them for Their Involvement

When I first started teaching, I was shocked to find out that there were parents who looked at school as the teacher's job and did not want to be involved or "mess things up." More often they thought that I was the professional in charge and it wasn't their place to tell me how to do my job or question me.

While that may sound refreshing at times, always deferring to the teacher isn't the best strategy for student success. Parents who meet with you can share something valuable about their child. They have often overcome several obstacles to be there, as well as built up their nerve. Thank them for their help and let them know that you value their input and see your relationship as a partnership on behalf of the student. Parents (including me!) want to feel like they are contributing to the solution, and if you allow them to, they very likely will have a positive influence.

Let's face it. Both parents and teachers can feel intimidated, inadequate, and like a scapegoat. It is so important, though, to push past those feeling and concentrate on what matters: the child. As a parent, I know that if a teacher is trying to help my child, I'll let a whole mountain of meaningless little pet peeves slide by. As a teacher, if I know a parent is championing his child, I'll shoulder some responsibility that I may not even feel is mine. Why? Because, as long as we are all fighting for the same thing, we don't all have to agree. If we just keep moving towards what the child needs, we'll all be able to celebrate the child's success together, as partners.

Your Turn

What can you do to involve parents in student learning?

- *Partnerships begin immediately.* What can you do to build a relationship with your students' families?
- *Really see every student.* What activities can you do or modify to help you understand your students better?
- *Share successes.* Is there a student who could really use a compliment or kind word? Make that happen. Remember, it doesn't have to be academic!
- *Acknowledge family expertise.* What questions can you ask to best learn about a particular student?
- *Go Team!* A meeting can be with any family member who might help, as well as school personnel. When meeting, create a plan and follow up. Don't be afraid to meet again.

A Final Thought...

Differentiation doesn't fit very well in a planbook, but then again, neither do our students. I'm an admitted Type A over-planner, but I fight those urges to control the process and product every day because I've learned that my students flourish with flexibility, and my inclinations towards order and organization are about me, not them. This wasn't an easy place to come to, as I was convinced for many years that the more work I did to plan out every segment of a lesson, anticipate every question, and predict which types of questions would be on "the assessment" (whichever one it was at the time), the better my students would be in the long run. And, for a while, this worked.

The problem is, the world changed very quickly. To put this into perspective, the year I was finishing my teaching certification is the year that my graduate school boyfriend set up an email account for me. My answer to his sweet gesture, "I see you everyday. Why would I want to write you a note on a computer?" It has been nearly twenty years, and this story is hilarious to my middle school students who will be building a website this quarter and can't imagine a world where constant communication was not only an option, but a prerequisite for many types of success.

Though I joke about this now, it can feel very risky to truly differentiate. It might require you to make a stand about your grading, take a position on standardized testing (or standardized anything, for that matter), and stick your neck out for your students in ways that you had not anticipated when you signed up for *Foundations of Educations*. I believe, though, that the same inclination that made you sign up for that first education class reveals itself in the little voice in your head that reminds you to teach children, not content, to assess progress, not test-taking aptitude, and to facilitate, not dominate. **Listen to that voice.**

Bibliography

Barnes, Mark. February 2016. Personal Interview.

Beck, I. L., McKeown, M. G. and Kucan, L. 2002. *Bringing Words to Life*. New York, NY: The Guilford Press.

Centers for Disease Control. November 23, 2013. "National Health Education Standards." www.cds.gov/healthyschools/index.htm.

Ferlazzo, Larry. May 2011. "Involvement or Engagement?" *Educational Leadership*. ASCD.

Friedman, Thomas. 2007. *The World Is Flat*. London, England: Picador.

Larmer, John, editor in chief. November 14, 2013. "Project Based Learning vs. Problem Based Learning vs. XBL." BIE.org.

Lenhart, Amanda. April 2015. "Teens, Social Media and Technology Overview 2015." Pew Research Center. Pewinternet.org.

Marzano, Robert J. 1992. *A Different Kind of Classroom: Teaching with Dimensions of Learning*. Alexandria, VA: Association for Supervision and Curriculum Development.

Tomlinson, Carol. 1999. *The Differentiated Classroom: Responding to the Needs of All Learners*. Alexandria, VA: Association for Supervision and Curriculum Development.

U.S. Department of Health and Human Services, Public Health Service National Institute of Child Health And Human Development. April 2000. "National Reading Panel Report." NIH Pub. No. 00–4754.

Wiggins, Grant and Jay McTighe. 2005. *Understanding by Design. 2nd ed.* Alexandria, VA: Association for Supervision and Curriculum Development.

Wong, Harry. 1991. *The First Days of School*. Mountain View, CA: Harry K. Wong Publications.

Wormeli, Rick. 2001. *Meet Me in the Middle: Becoming an Accomplished Middle-Level Teacher*. Portland, ME: Stenhouse Publishers.

Printed in the United States
by Baker & Taylor Publisher Services